"Sheela Raja writes with brilliant simplicity. *The Resilient Teen* is relatable and provides the reader with practical, manageable, and realistic steps. Raja joins with the reader in ways that promote individual hope and universal compassion. The message is loud and clear: being resilient is possible and *The Resilient Teen* lets us know how."

—**Susan A. Green, LCSW**, clinical professor, and codirector of The Institute on Trauma and Trauma-Informed Care at the University at Buffalo School of Social Work

"Using research and engaging stories, *The Resilient Teen* offers relevant, straightforward information about physical and emotional health. It provides practical guidance for managing sleep, stress, and difficult emotions, and tips for developing mindfulness, healthy habits, and social connections. The chapter on cognitive flexibility and realistic optimism, skills that can help transform difficult situations and lead to growth after hardship, make this book especially valuable and timely (for both adults and teens)."

—**Brigid McCaw, MD, MS, MPH**, clinical advisor for California Adverse Childhood Experiences (ACEs) Aware Initiative, and medical director (retired) at Kaiser Permanente Family Violence Prevention Program

"Sheela Raja has crafted a timely, practical, and substantive resource—not only for teens who are experiencing distress and adversity, but also for those who are seeking emotional well-being skills. It is developmentally appropriate, accessible, engaging, and beautifully written. Parents and professionals looking for an exceptional resource to promote resilience and adaptive functioning in teens will be thrilled with Raja's latest offering—arguably her best book to date."

—**Matt Gray, PhD**, professor of psychology at the University of Wyoming, trained at the National Center for PTSD, specializing in trauma

"This book is a gift to youth and for youth during a precarious time. When thoughts, emotions, and body sensations are in flux, a compassionate and stabilizing voice can ring like a bell of clarity to reach and heal the hurt. Speaking directly to teens and young adults, Raja provides practical skills to navigate the world, build resilience, and grow to lead a meaningful life. A pragmatic and insightful read!"

—**Roxana Cruz, MD, FACP**, director of medical and clinical affairs at the Texas Association of Community Health Centers, working with underserved and vulnerable populations

"If you're a teenager facing challenges of any kind, do a kind thing for yourself and download this book. Raja guides you toward bouncing back by asking gentle yet thought-provoking questions. The great mix of stories, science, and bite-sized, actionable steps makes it a nourishing read. But, as a longtime college counselor, I love that while you learn more about becoming resilient, you'll also learn more about yourself."

—**Arun Poonusamy**, chief academic officer of Collegewise,
and host of the *Get Wise* podcast

"Sheela Raja has written an important book that helps teens develop critical skills toward holistic emotional wellness. Raja offers clear definitions, relatable examples, and practical advice and strategies. Psychotherapists, youth workers, and teachers can use this as a guide in their work with individual teens and groups. I can see parents and teens using this book to foster rich mealtime dialogue while learning together."

—**Cynthia Lubin Langtiw, PsyD**, professor in the
clinical PsyD program at The Chicago School of
Professional Psychology, Chicago Campus

"Today's teens need resilience now more than ever. As everyone is grappling with questions about social justice and issues of public health, once again, Raja creates a clear, compassionate, and actionable plan for the adolescent. *The Resilient Teen* is filled with practical tips and tools to which teenagers will readily be able to relate. By normalizing the existence of stressors for everyone, Raja promotes thoughtful ideas for improved well-being and enhanced resilience. So logical and empathetic in her approach, Raja again demonstrates why she is a leader in the field of teen trauma and resilience. These will be valuable life lessons for the reader to take into adulthood!"

—**Shairi R. Turner, MD, MPH**, chief transformation officer
at Crisis Text Line; and CEO of Shairi Turner MD Coaching and
Consulting, LLC

the *i*nstant help solutions series

Young people today need mental health resources more than ever. That's why New Harbinger created the **Instant Help Solutions Series** especially for teens. Written by leading psychologists, physicians, and professionals, these evidence-based self-help books offer practical tips and strategies for dealing with a variety of mental health issues and life challenges teens face, such as depression, anxiety, bullying, eating disorders, trauma, and self-esteem problems.

Studies have shown that young people who learn healthy coping skills early on are better able to navigate problems later in life. Engaging and easy-to-use, these books provide teens with the tools they need to thrive—at home, at school, and on into adulthood.

This series is part of the **New Harbinger Instant Help Books** imprint, founded by renowned child psychologist Lawrence Shapiro. For a complete list of books in this series, visit newharbinger.com.

the resilient teen

10 key skills to **bounce back** from **setbacks** & **turn stress** into **success**

SHEELA RAJA, PhD

Instant Help Books
An Imprint of New Harbinger Publications, Inc.

SEP 0 7 2021

Publisher's Note

This publication is designed to provide accurate and authoritative information in regard to the subject matter covered. It is sold with the understanding that the publisher is not engaged in rendering psychological, financial, legal, or other professional services. If expert assistance or counseling is needed, the services of a competent professional should be sought.

INSTANT HELP, the Clock Logo, and NEW HARBINGER are trademarks of New Harbinger Publications, Inc.

Distributed in Canada by Raincoast Books

Copyright © 2021 by Sheela Raja
Instant Help Books
An imprint of New Harbinger Publications, Inc.
5674 Shattuck Avenue
Oakland, CA 94609
www.newharbinger.com

Cover design by Amy Shoup; Acquired by Tesilya Hanauer; Edited by Marisa Solis

Library of Congress Cataloging-in-Publication Data

Names: Raja, Sheela, author.
Title: The resilient teen : 10 key skills to bounce back from setbacks and turn stress into success / Sheela Raja, PhD.
Description: Oakland : New Harbinger Publications, 2021. | Series: The instant help solutions series | Includes bibliographical references.
Identifiers: LCCN 2020045385 (print) | LCCN 2020045386 (ebook) | ISBN 9781684035786 (trade paperback) | ISBN 9781684035793 (pdf) | ISBN 9781684035809 (epub)
Subjects: LCSH: Resilience (Personality trait) in adolescence--Juvenile literature. | Emotions--Juvenile literature. | Self-help techniques--Juvenile literature.
Classification: LCC BF724.3.R47 R35 2021 (print) | LCC BF724.3.R47 (ebook) | DDC 155.5/1824--dc23
LC record available at https://lccn.loc.gov/2020045385
LC ebook record available at https://lccn.loc.gov/2020045386

Printed in the United States of America

23 22 21

10 9 8 7 6 5 4 3 2 1   First Printing

For all the amazing teenagers,
and for two very special teenagers in my life—Leila and Jaya

Contents

Introduction

Thank you for picking up this book! There might be lots of reasons that you're thinking of reading a book on resilience. Maybe you're struggling with schoolwork, social pressures, or relationships, or you worry a lot about how uncertain the future might feel. Or maybe you've experienced something really difficult like discrimination or some kind of violence in your life, and you're trying to find ways to survive and thrive. Maybe you feel like you are doing okay right now, but you want to find ways to feel happier and more relaxed, have better relationships with your friends and family, and feel more energetic and motivated.

Stressors, or the things that cause you to be stressed out, are an unavoidable part of life. Obstacles never stop coming!

But wait, you may be thinking, *lots of people seem to have their act together! Why can't I get my life together?* Scientists have asked this same question, and they've identified many skills that can help you deal with stress and setbacks. And that's what this book is about: teaching you how to become more resilient.

Resilience skills can help you enjoy the good times and learn how to cope with the stressful times. They will help you feel motivated, energized, and connected, and they help you create a life you truly love. They can give you the strength you need to form deeper relationships, get more involved in your community, and help make the world a better place.

As you try out the skills in this book, see what fits you best—based on your routine, interests, and personality. Your journey is unique and important, and you'll find plenty of ways to personalize your path to resilience.

What Is Resilience?

The dictionary lists two definitions of "resilience." The first focuses on how a physical body, including cells in our body, can retain its shape after being compressed. The second addresses how people respond to stress.

---

re·sil·ience (Merriam-Webster 2020g)

1: The capability of a strained body to recover its size and shape after deformation caused especially by compressive stress.

2: An ability to recover from or adjust easily to misfortune or change.

This book is focused on the second definition. Basically, you can think of resilience as your *ability to adapt during times of stress or change.*

There are a lot of misconceptions about what resilience really means in psychology and health. Let's start with what resilience is not. Being resilient doesn't mean that you are always calm and happy. You're human—you'll have feelings and emotions during times of stress. You'll even experience negative, difficult, and painful emotions that at times seem overwhelming. That's perfectly normal!

The interesting thing about resilience is that it makes room for you to experience negative emotions *and* find ways to survive and thrive in your life. Resilience can happen right along with difficult emotions. Resilience is about having the good times with the bad, and learning to cope when you fall down. *Resilience isn't a destination, it's an approach to life.*

And resilience can be learned—you aren't born with it. So by learning and practicing the skills in this book, you can develop resilience. By doing things every day to keep your mind, body, and spirit healthy, you can make yourself more ready to deal with stressful times.

Think of it this way: if you suddenly find yourself needing to run two miles, it's going to be a lot easier if you've practiced sprinting short distances ahead of time. That's the approach of this book—start building up healthy habits in small ways so that when you need them the most, you've already had some practice.

As you read this book, the following definition might be the most useful way to think about resilience.

---

re·sil·ience

1: A set of skills that help you develop a healthy mind and body.

2: Techniques that help you develop strong and healthy emotional connections and a sense of purpose.

3: A set of practices that help you cope in healthy ways during times of stress.

Why Learn Resilience Skills?

In an ideal world, we wouldn't need books like this one. There would be no stress or misfortune. No one would experience setbacks. Unfortunately, we don't live in an ideal world. If you've been through times when you feel very worried about things, you're not alone. Life is full of daily stressors that may cause you difficult emotions like anxiety, sadness, or anger.

For example, you might worry about taking a test, meeting new people, trying out for a sport or club, or starting a new school year. We can often manage these short-term stressors, but if they happen all at once, it can be tough on us. According to the American Psychological

Association (2018), many teens experience stress associated with the following situations or places:

- School and work
- Getting into a good college or deciding what to do after high school
- Family finances
- Relationships with parents and family
- Problems with friends and romantic partners
- Family responsibilities

It's not uncommon to feel worried or down if you move to a new neighborhood, or if there is a divorce or separation in your family. These kinds of stressors are not that different from the generations that came before you. People have always worried about money, work, and relationships. For example, 81 percent of young people between the ages of eighteen and twenty-one report money as a source of significant stress. And 63 percent of young people fifteen to seventeen report that their families not having enough money is a significant source of stress (American Psychological Association 2018).

When all age groups are included, many people report being worried about violence and crime, their health and health care, hate crimes, wars or conflict, terrorist attacks in the United States, taxes, controversies or scandals, and unemployment or low wages. Depending on their ethnicity and sexual orientation, about 10 to 30 percent of people also report that discrimination is a significant source of stress in their life.

Your generation has some additional sources of stress (American Psychological Association 2018). Young people have been highly affected by issues facing our nation, including financial and social uncertainty, gun violence, and public health issues.

Some key facts about people ages twenty-one and younger:

- 33 percent are worried about their personal debt, including things like loans.

- 31 percent are worried about housing instability, meaning they don't always have a reliable, safe place to live.

- 28 percent worry about food insecurity, meaning that they some-times don't have enough to eat or lack the resources to obtain healthy or nutritious food on a regular basis.

- 69 percent feel "significantly stressed" about our nation's future.

- 75 percent report mass shootings as a significant source of stress.

When you look at the prevalence of all of these worries and stressors, it's easy to feel overwhelmed. But what it really means is that you aren't alone. Many people struggle with significant obstacles, and we have a lot to learn from those who successfully overcome them. You can learn ways to approach life in a resilient way. There are many skills that can help you navigate difficult situations, and that is what this book is about.

Your Generation Wants Help

If you feel that you've experienced periods of stress, depression, or anxiety, you aren't alone (American Psychological Association 2018). Let's look at more key facts:

- 27 percent of young people below the age of twenty-one (some-times called Generation Z) report their mental health as fair or poor (compared to millennials, 15 percent; Generation Xers, 13 percent; baby boomers, 7 percent; older adults, 5 percent).

- Young people are more likely than some other generations to report that they have been diagnosed with an anxiety disorder (18 percent) and more likely than all other generations to be diagnosed with depression (23 percent).

It could be that the increased awareness of mental health and reduced stigma has made your generation more willing to report mental health problems, and this has led to an increased willingness to actually seek help.

Overall, younger generations are significantly more likely to receive or have received treatment or therapy from a psychologist or other mental health professional (American Psychological Association 2018). In fact, as we will talk about often in this book, seeking help is a key resilience skill. So just by picking up this book, you're already on the way.

Trauma and Toxic Stress

In addition, some teens face more serious or traumatic stressors, including bullying, chronic illness, interpersonal and sexual violence, and other kinds of abuse. Sadly, many teens don't always feel safe at home or in their own neighborhoods, sometimes witnessing family or community violence.

Some teens may have experienced sexual or physical abuse, often from someone they know, like a family member, friend, or dating partner (Wincentak, Connolly, and Card 2017). Bullying is also an issue that we are taking a lot more seriously in recent years, because it can really affect you (Kann et al. 2018).

When traumatic events happen repeatedly, it's called *toxic stress*—the kind of stress that can take a serious toll on your mental and physical health (Shonkoff et al. 2012). If that's the case for you, don't give up hope. The resilience skills in this book may be particularly helpful as you try to create the life you want and deserve. It's a good idea to pay special attention to part III, "Engaging with the World Around You Every Day," for ways to find a trusted adult (a teacher, counselor, family member, or someone else) to help you develop these resilience skills.

Help for Toxic Stress: Joey's Story

Joey is a thirteen-year-old in eighth grade. His parents divorced several years ago, and his mom's boyfriend recently moved into the house. Joey has a lot of responsibilities at home, including having to take care of his little brother and sister after school.

His mother's boyfriend is currently unemployed, and instead of helping take care of the family, he drinks alcohol and often yells at Joey for "being stupid and wasting time." Joey's grades begin to slip and he finds himself losing his self-confidence. He even starts to stutter at school, causing his classmates to make fun of him.

One day, a teacher pulls Joey aside and asks him about his grades. She's kind in her approach, and instead of accusing Joey, she wants to know if everything is okay. Joey decides to take a leap of faith and trust his teacher. He tells her about the recent changes at home and how it is affecting him. The teacher contacts the school social worker, and they begin to talk to Joey's mom about some ways to improve their life at home. Although nothing changes overnight, Joey's decision not to struggle alone is really important for his future.

Post-Traumatic Growth

Some people who have experienced serious stressors eventually find opportunities for *post-traumatic growth*. Over time, these people find that the difficult situations give them a chance to form new, more meaningful relationships, find a deeper appreciation and purpose in life, and help them recognize how strong they really are (Tedeschi et al. 2018). This does not mean being happy that you experienced these terrible situations. Not at all. It simply means that you have the potential to learn and grow from them.

Post-traumatic growth is closely related to resilience. You can think of resilience as finding ways to survive and adapt under stress, while post-traumatic growth is a way to find meaning in what you've experienced. In parts III and IV of this book, "Engaging with the World Around You Every Day" and "Finding Meaning, Joy, and Purpose," you'll learn important skills for post-traumatic growth and resilience.

Resilience Skills Are a Way of Life

Resilience skills will help you face short-term pressures and disappointment. They can also teach you to survive and thrive after longer-term, more serious stressors. Resilience isn't a destination, it's an approach to life. These skills are based on the latest research from psychology, public health, and neuroscience, and they are divided into the four parts of this book:

Part I: Caring for Your Physical Health. Part I will give you suggestions about how to form a routine that works for you, without being boring. We will also discuss how to realistically face unhealthy coping (for example, substance abuse) in a way that doesn't make you feel ashamed or criticized.

Part II: Caring for Your Mental and Emotional Heath. Part II will focus on mindfulness, which is the ability to focus on what is happening in the present moment—rather than being overly focused on the past or the future. We will also explore how to deal with difficult emotions, including depression and anxiety, and how to learn from your past when making future plans.

Part III: Engaging with the World Around You Every Day. Part III explores how to form safe connections and build a strong support system. We will also experiment with ways to take healthy chances and see how that relates to your relationships and feelings about yourself.

Part IV: Finding Meaning, Joy, and Purpose. Part IV will explore ways to create realistic optimism in situations. We will talk about how humor, community service, and activism might all play a role in finding more meaning in your life.

Although the skills in this book can (and should) be practiced with short-term stressors, they are also effective in longer-term and highly stressful situations. Remember that resilience doesn't mean you will be symptom-less or stress-free. People can still find joy and meaning in their lives while also experiencing some difficult emotions.

As of this writing, the world is facing the huge challenge of the COVID-19 pandemic. Resilience skills are more important than ever. To see how the techniques in this book apply to the challenges of social distancing and dealing with uncertainty, you can access supplemental

information for free at this book's website, http://www.newharbinger
.com/45786.

Your past does not have to define your future. Maybe you feel that
you haven't dealt with stress in the best ways. Maybe you've experienced
a lot of difficult things in your life. You can start now and find ways to
learn, survive, and thrive. As you go through this book, keep an open
mind and try to experiment with various techniques until you find the
right fit for you. You are starting a journey of creating a healthier, happier
lifestyle. Think of yourself as a scientist, an explorer, an entrepreneur, an
artist, or an athlete—and start creating your own personalized resilience
recipe!

PART I

Caring for Your Physical Health

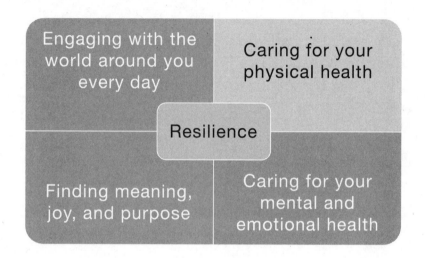

Engaging with the world around you every day

Caring for your physical health

Resilience

Finding meaning, joy, and purpose

Caring for your mental and emotional health

Finding a Routine: Sleep, Diet, Exercise, and Technology

When you think about the word "routine," you probably think of the adjective "boring." Well, that's at least partially true. But a good routine is a key building block of resilience. You need a predictable way to take care of yourself, especially when it comes to sleeping, eating, exercise, and screen time. These elements are the foundation of your health and feeling good. And you probably have experienced that when one of these elements is out of balance, so are you.

Your body works best when it's in a calm, predictable environment. Basically, a regular amount of sleep, plus healthy doses of exercise and nutrition, help keep us going. And the hidden benefit of routines is that they actually give us the fuel to be more spontaneous and have more fun. Your body can more easily adapt to short-term stress (for example, cramming for an exam) if you are fueled and rested, and you're also more likely to be able to stay up late talking to your friends on the weekend if you aren't tired all week.

Some of the skills in this section might seem very basic, but you might actually find that minor changes to your routine bring you some really great benefits. A good routine can help you feel better physically and emotionally, which makes stress more manageable and good times more enjoyable.

Keeping Your Body Calm

You might be wondering why a routine is so important. Basically, it goes back to the way our bodies are wired. Our bodies are meant to deal with short-term stressors. Think about a caveman running away from a tiger. When the man sees the tiger, what happens? His *sympathetic nervous system* begins to work, and the *fight-or-flight response* immediately kicks in, which means that his body is getting ready to either run away from the tiger or fight with it. During the fight-or-flight response, our heart rate increases (for more energy), our pupils dilate (for better vision), and our digestion slows down. In addition, there is something called the *hypothalamic-pituitary-adrenal (HPA) axis* that is activated during stress. Basically, the adrenal glands start a process that signals the body to produce stress hormones, including cortisol. These hormones increase our blood pressure and our blood sugar so that we can deal with stressful situations.

Once the stress is over (the tiger is killed or it's outrun), it takes a few minutes—sometimes twenty or more minutes—for the body to calm down. In general, our bodies are built to deal with short-terms stressors, but only if we are already fueled and rested. If you have a good routine most of the time, it will be a lot easier to bounce back from short-term stressors that upset your body. That's why sleep, diet, and exercise are so important.

Finding a Sleep Routine

One of the most important things you can do for yourself is to establish a good sleeping routine. It's very common for teens to feel as if they aren't getting enough sleep. There may be so many demands on your time—homework, clubs, sports, or an afterschool job. In addition, maybe when you finally try to sleep you are kept awake worrying about what's going to happen tomorrow.

If you're not sleeping well, it's very hard to concentrate, manage your mood, or feel energized. And if life throws an unexpected stressor your way, it's even harder to manage when you are aren't well rested.

Try to create an environment that is safe, calm, and *predictable*. We are all creatures of habit. By creating a familiar routine that is associated with sleep, we learn—usually over the course of several weeks—that certain places and patterns are associated with rest. It's okay to deviate from the routine once a week or so, but for the most part, your sleep routine should be the same every day. Here are some sleep basics you should try to put into place most of the time:

SLEEP INVENTORY

1. Do you go to sleep at around the same time every night (give or take 45 minutes)?

   → If you answered no, consider trying to go to bed around the same time every night, for at least four nights a week. Don't worry if you can't fall asleep right away. The important thing is to allow yourself some time to get used to a new routine.

2. Do you wake up at the same time every morning (give or take 45 minutes)?

   → If you answered no, consider setting an alarm to wake up around the same time, for at least four mornings a week. You can expect that you will be somewhat sleepy for the first week. But eventually, waking up and going to sleep at the same time will become a routine.

3. Is the place you sleep quiet?

    → If you answered no, think about what kinds of noise you can control. Can you turn off or turn down the volume of electronic devices? Do you need to wear earplugs? Do you need some neutral background noise? Some people like falling asleep to white noise, like radio static, while others prefer recordings of calming noises.

4. Do you use technology within one hour of going to bed?

    → If you answered yes, think about limiting your use of technology. Technology often emits light, particularly blue light, which can interfere with the hormones needed for sleep (including melatonin). If at all possible, try to stay off of electronics at least one hour before bed, at least several days a week. If this seems too difficult, start with a half an hour of tech-free time before sleep. Even small steps can help.

5. Do you sleep with technology around you (computer or phone by your bed)?

    → If you answered yes, think about limiting your use of technology. Again, the blue light emitted by technology interferes with your sleep hormones. In addition, the buzzing sounds of incoming texts can interfere with your sleep. If you need an alarm to wake up, try buying an old-fashioned alarm clock (yes, they still sell those).

6. Do you have things in your sleeping environment that cause you stress (for example, textbooks or clutter)?

    → If you answered yes, try to find ways to make your sleeping environment more soothing. For example, if looking at your textbook or computer gives you stress about tomorrow, see if you can move those things into a nearby hallway. The area where you sleep should be a sanctuary, decorated in colors you like, with objects that give you happiness.

Don't worry if you can't do these things every day. No routine is perfect. But keep in mind that it takes at least eight weeks to form new habits. So keep trying, and aim for at least four to five days a week.

Once you start working on your sleep routine, you might find that you need help with actually falling asleep. Here are two techniques you can use before bed to help you fall asleep.

PROGRESSIVE MUSCLE RELAXATION FOR SLEEP

Progressive muscle relaxation is a technique that involves tightening and then relaxing your muscles, which helps you let go of tension in your body. None of the movements should be painful, so you can skip any muscle groups that you find difficult. You can repeat each set of tensing and relaxing two to three times for the best effects.

When you are lying down in bed, take a few deep breaths before you get started.

1. Flex your toes toward your head. Feel them stretch. Now let them come back to their natural position. Feel the arches of your feet relax and feel your toes come back to their resting position. Feel the difference between the tension and the relaxation.

2. Tighten your calf muscles by flexing your toes up toward your head. Now let go and feel your ankle and calf muscles come back to a resting position.

3. Tighten your glute muscles. As you relax them, feel how your lower back and legs also release tension.

4. Take a deep breath and feel your stomach and chest expand. As you exhale, feel them let go and relax. Take another breath, and this time exhale as much as you can, pulling your stomach muscles in toward your spine. As you take your next breath, feel the natural rhythm of your stomach and chest muscles as they relax.

5. Push your shoulders up toward your ears. Now slowly let your shoulders come back to their resting position. Feel the difference between the tension and the natural, relaxed position of your shoulders.

6. Make a fist with both of your hands. As you let go, feel your wrists and fingers relax. Make a silly face by smiling and showing all of your teeth (don't worry, no one will notice). As you let go, feel the corners of your mouth relax.

7. Shut your eyes tightly. Now slowly open your eyes. Feel your eyelids and cheek muscles let go and relax.

8. Tighten or flex all of the muscle groups at the same time. You can flex your toes, take a deep breath, push up your shoulders, tighten your fists, and close your eyes tightly. As you let go, feel the difference in the muscle groups throughout your body.

People who have tension in their bodies usually like progressive muscle relaxation. However, if it is your mind that holds a lot of stress, you might want to try the next exercise, which focuses on a way to create calmer thoughts. If you have a good imagination, this exercise is for you.

GUIDED IMAGERY FOR SLEEP

Take a few deep breaths and gently close your eyes. Imagine a setting that is totally your own and relaxing, safe, and nurturing in every way. You are in total control here. Maybe you are on a beach, in the mountains, with friends, in your home, or somewhere else.

Look around and see everything in detail. What are the colors? Are there any sounds? Take a minute and hear them. Pay attention to how your surroundings smell.

Now imagine yourself walking around your safe space. Maybe you pick something up—a soft blanket or a handful of sand—anything that gives you comfort. Take a few minutes and really enjoy the scene you have created. You can go there anytime you want. This is your personal retreat when life feels stressful.

You can experiment with doing this exercise at different times of the day until you find a time that works well for you. You can try it when you are lying down and ready to go sleep, or you can try it after you are done with your homework for the day. See what works best for you.

Diet and Exercise

Once your sleep routine is predictable (and maybe a little boring), the next thing to focus on is your diet and exercise. You want to make sure you're giving your body plenty of predictability to deal with unpredictable parts of life—both good and bad. This way, when you have an unexpected deadline at school or a chance to spend a fun weekend with a friend, you know your body will feel up to the challenge—and not overly tired or run-down.

There's a biological reason that diet and exercise matter. When you are stressed, your body goes through a complex process that gets you ready to fight off infection. But that process can lead to inflammation—characterized by heat, swelling, and pain—which isn't good for your body in the long term. Healthy, nutritious foods and moderate exercise actually reduce inflammation. That way, if you are fighting a short-term infection or stressor, your body isn't already exhausted and inflamed. That's why diet and exercise are an important part of resilience.

Many teens reach for sugary sodas, energy drinks, and junk food for an energy boost (or just for fun). This diet might work for a few days, but you've probably noticed that you start to feel sluggish after a while. Although the quick boost to your blood sugar works in the short term, it won't keep you energized enough to stay up late every night working on a project that might take several weeks.

Similarly, just sitting on the sofa looking at your phone might help you feel entertained or distracted for a few hours, but if that's your routine day after day, your body might start to feel stiff and tired. A good diet and exercise routine can help you feel energized in all parts of your life, including while sitting in class, doing homework, or keeping up with responsibilities at home or at work.

A diet and exercise routine doesn't mean you can't have any fun. In general, try to stick to a healthy food and exercise schedule for four or five days, followed by a few days of less structure. For example, you might want to plan to have a routine for eating and exercise on the weekdays, and allow your weekends to be a little more spontaneous.

Why a Routine Matters: Maya's Story

Maya is a junior in high school, and her school switched to online learning because of the coronavirus pandemic. Because of the social distancing measures, Maya was unable to participate in her clubs or hang out with her friends. Basically, she went from a schedule that was really busy to days with no structure at all. After a few weeks of eating junk food, having no gym class, and going to bed really late, Maya felt like she couldn't concentrate on e-learning. She didn't text her friends as much.

As the weeks went on, Maya and her family realized that the pandemic wasn't a short-term stressor—the quarantine might last for months. The family was going to have to find a way to create a new routine in order to feel healthy. To help her get out of the slump, Maya made a simple list of a few easy things she needed to do before noon. Her list was realistic. She decided that she had to get up at 10 a.m. on weekdays and eat some toast and fruit for breakfast. She also decided that she needed to go out to her small backyard right after breakfast and take a few deep breaths.

These minor changes helped Maya feel healthier for the rest of the day. Although she still ate some junk food, she was more likely to eat a healthy lunch and do her homework on the days she got up and ate breakfast. A little bit of routine went a long way in helping Maya during a very uncertain time.

The first step to setting up a diet and exercise routine is to pay attention to what you are doing now, and then set up some small, manageable goals.

MONITOR YOUR DIET AND ACTIVITY

Use a piece of paper or your phone to keep track of your diet and exercise habits for one week. At the end of every day, write down the answers to each of the following questions:

1. How many fruits and vegetables did you eat?

2. How much junk food did you eat (chips, candy bars, soft drinks)?

3. How much fast food did you eat?

4. Did you get a half hour of exercise (gym class, yoga, sports, brisk walking)?

After the week is over, come up with two goals focused on healthy eating and exercise. The key is to make these goals small and attainable. For example, instead of eating chips after school, try to eat fruit two days a week. Or maybe your goal is to start your morning with a few yoga stretches on Monday, Wednesday, and Friday. Make sure your goals are small and specific. And put them on your calendar!

Now that you have come up with a few goals, the final step is to figure out how you are going to keep yourself motivated. This book has lots of suggestions around motivation, and here is an exercise to start.

BE YOUR OWN CHEERING SECTION

This exercise focuses on the things we say to ourselves. Whether we realize it or not, we are always talking to ourselves! That's perfectly normal. *Self-talk* can be an important tool in helping us make positive changes. Sometimes we talk ourselves into things we do (or do not) want to do, and sometimes we can be pretty tough on ourselves.

When you are trying to make changes in your diet and exercise, you will have bad days and good days. Learn to use positive self-talk to keep you on task and motivated.

- **Congratulate your efforts.** When you are having a good day, learn how to congratulate yourself. Develop a few statements that focus on the specific skills you used. For example, "I did a good job by planning my snack and packing it ahead of time," or "I'm glad I took time out to play a game of basketball with my friends."

- **Don't beat yourself up.** When you're having a bad day, learn how to say things to yourself that focus on the future, not the past. For example, "It's okay that I ate a lot of cake today. Tomorrow I'll focus on eating a few more fruits and vegetables." This is being compassionate with yourself, just like you'd be with a good friend.

- **Post it.** Put some of these *positive statements* into your phone or write them on sticky notes and post them in visible spots. Pretty soon they will become a part of how you think.

Living with Technology

We can't discuss your daily routine without talking about technology! Computers, tablets, and smartphones are an essential part of our lives. But we need to find ways to make this technology work for us, instead of letting our online life dominate our thoughts and free time. According to the American Psychological Association, younger generations are experiencing more mental health issues than previous generations. Although they're more willing to talk openly about their struggles, they're not always finding support (American Psychological Association 2018).

- 73 percent say they could have used more emotional support in the past year.

- 55 percent report that social media provides feelings of support, but 45 percent also report feeling judged on social media, and 38 percent say that social media makes them feel bad about themselves.

Where Do I Fit In? Justin's Story

Justin is a seventeen-year-old senior. As many of his friends get ready to go off to college or trade school, he feels lost. He has never been a great student, and he honestly doesn't know what he wants to do after graduation. He feels like he's the only person who doesn't have his future figured out.

In the second semester of senior year, Justin finds himself caring less and less about classes. He oversleeps and often skips breakfast and lunch. He spends a lot of time on social media in hopes of connecting with people who are also feeling the same way. Instead, he sees many posts about how excited people are about the future and how much they're going to miss all their high school friends. Justin even posts, "Anyone else feel like life after high school isn't that great?" He's crushed when his post only gets a few likes.

Social media, when used well, can really help you feel connected and close to other people. But it can also make you feel lonely and isolated. Thinking about what kind of limits you want to set for yourself is an important resilience skill. To do this means setting up a routine whereby technology is a part of your life, but not all of your life.

We live in a culture that is obsessed with posting things publicly and doing things for likes. You can choose how much you want to participate in this. Later sections of this book will focus on creating trusting relationships and finding meaning and purpose in your life. As you do that, you might find that your time online naturally declines or changes. Until that time, the first step is to set some manageable limits for yourself.

DON'T LET TECHNOLOGY BOSS YOU AROUND

You might want to cut back on your use of technology if:

- Separating from your phone or device causes you anxiety.

- You consistently spend time on your device and pass up opportunities to get involved in activities or go out with friends.

- You constantly check your device in social situations.

- You have difficulty sleeping if your device is not next to you.

- You become easily distracted during class or when people are talking.

- You find yourself becoming sad or anxious after using social media.

Some ways to consider limiting your use include:

- **Do not sleep with your phone** or other electronic device. If you need an alarm, use an old-fashioned alarm clock.

- **Install an app that helps you set limits** on your social networking time. Try to limit yourself to less than an hour a day. If that seems impossible, start with a limit of two hours.

- **Do not use any technology an hour before bed.** If that seems impossible, start with no technology half an hour before you go to sleep.

- **Set aside at least half an hour a day that is technology-free.** This could be at meals, when walking to school or work, or while doing something fun. Put away *all* the technology for a short time and allow yourself to become totally immersed in whatever you are doing. Eventually, try to increase your tech-free time to at least an hour a day.

Putting the Skills Together: Katy's Busy Schedule

Katy is fifteen years old and active on her school's track team. She's an honors student and is friends with many kinds of people, although during track season she has little opportunity to socialize with friends who aren't on the team. Other people think she has it all.

The problem is that when Katy's track season is over, she finds it difficult to stick to any sort of routine. She eats lots of junk food as soon as track ends, which leaves her feeling low in energy. In addition, she finds herself online late at night texting her friends. Katy also feels like she has to "make up for lost time" whenever she can, so she goes out more often and stays up late.

There are many options Katy has to set a healthier routine. She can tackle her diet, her technology usage, or her sleep routine. In this case, she decides that texting her friends is important to her.

However, she starts by not taking her phone into her bedroom for three nights a week. When her sleep improves, she becomes more convinced that limiting her technology usage before bed is helpful.

Katy also begins to realize that it is normal that she wants to relax a little bit after an intense track season. She decides to include a little bit of junk food in her lunch every day, but decides not to eat chips and cookies as a meal. To keep herself motivated, Katy learns to tell herself, "I'm allowed to indulge myself because I work so hard. But I still want to stay healthy." Overall, Katy finds gentle, small changes that help her feel more rested and energized.

Resiliency Recap

Yes, a good routine might be a bit boring. But it's the boring part that is going to help you feel healthier, have more fun, and be able to respond better during times of stress. A routine is basically like filling up the gas tank in your car once a week. If you make that a habit, you'll be able to take that unexpected road trip with fewer stops!

As you consider a routine, think about your sleep habits, diet, exercise, and technology use. Try to keep your goals as realistic and specific as possible, be generous with yourself when you slip up, and make sure to stop and enjoy the sights along the way. You deserve it!

Face Unhealthy Habits

During your teen years, you'll learn ways of coping that will probably stay with you for a lifetime. The good news is that you'll have the chance to build up those healthy habits right now. If you have started coping in some unhealthy ways, it's not too late to change.

This skill focuses on some things you might prefer not to talk about openly, especially in front of adults. Teens don't always see the big picture when it comes to using alcohol or drugs, and smoking or vaping. You may think, *I'm just doing this once in a while,* or *I'm not really hurting myself.* The problem is, if these habits build up, they become a lot more difficult to change when you're older.

It's normal for teens to feel curious about experimenting with tobacco, drugs, and alcohol. You might have tried drinking or smoking cannabis because you wanted to see what they were like. You might be using alcohol or vaping to help your body relax. Maybe you want to feel less stressed, or maybe you want people to like you. Maybe something that started as a random social habit is now affecting your daily life.

The bottom line is that using alcohol or drugs, or smoking or vaping, are habits that might work fine in the short term, but they don't work well over time—especially when you are using them to cope with difficult feelings. Over months and years, your habit can turn into substance abuse, damaging both your emotional and your physical health. In this section you'll learn how to face habits that might be unhealthy and discover other ways to cope and enjoy yourself.

Tobacco, Alcohol, and Prescription and Nonprescription Drugs

Fortunately, rates of alcohol and drug use have declined in the last forty years (Johnston et al. 2017). Nevertheless, tobacco, alcohol, and prescription and nonprescription drug use are still common among teens. We won't cover all the ways drinking and using are bad for you—you're probably already aware of most of those issues. But what you might find interesting to know is that teens who use substances regularly are less likely to show resilience after stressful situations (Johnston et al. 2017). That's why it's so important to talk about this issue honestly and see whether you are using substances to deal with stress in your life.

Alcohol and Stress: Emma's Story

Emma is a sophomore in high school and active in several service clubs. She's also active in the student council and is hoping to major in English and film studies when she goes to college. Emma's made of lot of new friends through her clubs and activities. Some of the parties she is invited to have alcohol—mostly beer—when someone's parents are out to dinner for the night. Emma sometimes drinks a few beers at a party, and since she can walk home from most of the parties, she's not worried about driving while drunk.

As the year goes on, Emma discovers that her biology class is really difficult. She feels that her teacher thinks she's not that smart, and no matter how much she studies, she is getting Cs or Ds on her tests. Emma starts to worry that she's not going to get into college, and her anxiety starts to build up over the semester. So she starts to drink a beer or two by herself on weeknights. It helps her worry less about the future. Part of Emma realizes that her drinking is no longer social, that it's more about helping her deal with difficult emotions.

It can be hard to tell the difference between *substance use* that is social and *substance abuse* that is getting in the way of your ability to function. Part of the reason that it's so hard to distinguish them is because substance use is so common among young people. Among teenagers, by twelfth grade:

- About 25 percent have used marijuana at least once.

- 42 percent have consumed alcohol (more than a few sips), and 26 percent have been drunk.

- 18 percent have used cigarettes, and 27 percent have used e-vaporizers.

- 14 percent of teens have used prescription medications (such as opioids like oxycodone or Vicodin, and amphetamines like Adderall) for nonmedical purposes (Miech et al. 2017).

It can be hard to figure out whether your substance use is something you should be concerned about. The next exercise will help you decide whether you need help.

DO I NEED HELP?

Answer these questions as honestly as you can. This journey is all about learning how to take good care of yourself so you can bounce back when life sends you a curveball.

- When you socialize with your friends, is drinking or marijuana often involved?

- Have you ever had more than four drinks at one time?

- Do you smoke cigarettes or vape regularly?

- Have you ever used prescription drugs in a way that was not prescribed by your doctor (used someone else's prescription, taken too much of your own prescription, or taken a prescription after it was no longer medically required)?

- Have you ever used heroin, inhalants, tranquilizers, hallucinogens, or other illegal drugs?

- Have you ever gotten in trouble at work, school, or home because of substance use?

- Has substance use ever gotten in the way of you attending work or school, or taking care of your responsibilities?

→ If you answered yes to any of these questions, you should consider seeking help. Now is the time to change these habits. While it is normal to experiment with trying alcohol or tobacco occasionally in social settings, some behaviors (for example, drinking four or more drinks at a time, misusing prescription medication, or experimenting with substances like heroin, or inhalants) suggest you are at higher risk for substance abuse in the future.

Find a trusted adult to talk to—a family member, friend, teacher, counselor, or coach. If you are not sure who to trust, part III of this book has some exercises focused on how to find and sustain a healthy support system. In addition, the Resources section at the end of this book has more information about where you can start. If you have picked up this book, it's because you want to make a commitment to creating a great life for yourself. Reaching out for help will be an important part of your journey.

If substance use has become a problem for you, you'll need to find safe and healthy ways to have fun. And since you can't take something out of your routine without replacing it with something else, we'll look at how to develop a good self-care routine. A key resilience skill is developing healthy self-care habits.

WAYS TO RELAX

Find something you enjoy doing and try to do it every single day. There isn't one activity that fits everyone. The list is endless. Here are some suggestions:

- Walking, doing yoga, riding a bike, or playing sports

- Drawing, painting, or crafting

- Listening to music, singing, or playing an instrument

- Talking to your friends

- Writing letters, short stories, or poems

- Doing your hair or makeup

- Playing video games

- Taking a relaxing bath or shower

- Reading

- Cooking or baking

- Taking photographs

Generate at least one idea of how to take care of yourself. You can do the same thing every day, or you can keep trying new things. As long as you are focusing on things that are healthy for your body, there are no right or wrong answers. Basically, the more healthy ways you have to take care of yourself, the less likely you'll be to use substances as a way to cope with the stressful times in life.

Once you have started to take better care of yourself, you can cut back on the things that aren't good for you. If you have experimented with alcohol, tobacco, or drugs in social situations, it's important to learn strategies to prioritize your health and safety, so that experimentation does not turn into substance abuse in the future.

HARM REDUCTION

It's normal to experiment with substances. But when life gets stressful in the short or long term, you're more likely to be resilient if you have other ways to cope. Since so many teens occasionally use substances, you'll probably be in situations where you need to figure out how to keep yourself safe. You'll have to think about what is social—and what is dangerous. Here are some suggestions to keep yourself safer in situations that involve drugs, alcohol, or tobacco:

- **Drive safely.** Don't get into a car with someone who is under the influence of drugs or alcohol, and don't drive if you have used any substance.

- **Leave, if needed.** If you're in a place where drugs and alcohol are present, and you feel personally uncomfortable with the amount of use (for example, a lot of drunk people), try to leave the situation. If you can't leave, contact a trusted adult to help you.

- **Limit your use in social situations.** A common benchmark is to consume no more than two alcoholic drinks in any social situation, such as at a party. Of course, it's even better if you don't drink at all, but setting reasonable limits is one step toward making healthier choices related to your substance use.

- **Avoid sexual activity when using alcohol or drugs.** If you have consumed alcohol or any other substance, limit any romantic or sexual activity. Remember that you are not thinking clearly; people cannot consent when they are under the influence.

- **Be selective about friends.** If you have friends who smoke or drink regularly, try to limit or stop partying with them. You can still remain friendly and hang out in other settings, such as at school, in sports, or at club events. (See part III for more on forming trusting and safe relationships.)

- **Check in with your feelings.** Don't use drugs, alcohol, or tobacco when you are feeling anxious or depressed. When you use substances to cope with difficult feelings, it creates a cycle of dependency that can lead to addiction.

So what do you do instead? When you have healthier coping options, definitely turn to those. If you don't have them now, work on finding some and building them into your routines. Until you do that, your goal is to take steps to keep yourself as safe as possible.

When life gets stressful, you want to have plenty of ways to cope that are good for your body and your long-term goals. While substance use might work in the short term, resilient people rely on healthy habits to really get them through the tough times.

Putting the Skills Together: Ashley Struggles in School

Ashely is a quiet and artistic sixteen-year-old who is struggling to pass several of her classes. She is extremely worried about her grades and about what she is going to do after high school. She has a friend who uses amphetamines to help her stay more focused during class. Ashley asks her friend for a few extra pills.

After taking them for a couple of weeks, Ashley feels great. However, after about a month, Ashley begins to struggle with nightmares and starts to feel anxious and on edge most of the time. She worries that if she stops taking the amphetamines, her grades will drop again, but she also knows that she can't live with this level of anxiety.

Ashley decides she wants to stop using amphetamines, so she tries to avoid the friend who has supplied her with the pills. After about a week without the amphetamines, Ashley is irritable and exhausted every morning. She summons all of her courage and confides in her older sister, who is in college, and asks for help. Ashley's sister tells her parents, and although they're angry, the family starts to work with the school psychologist and guidance counselor to help Ashley cope with her grades, her anxiety, and her parents' divorce.

Ashley and her psychologist discuss ways to deal with stress and how to tackle anxiety about the future. Ashley begins to paint and draw again, something she had stopped doing after she and her mom moved to their new apartment. Although it's only a small step, it makes Ashley feel that things might eventually feel normal again.

Many of Ashley's new choices will support her long-term resilience. Trusting her instincts, limiting contact with the friend who supplied the pills, and being honest about her substance abuse were extremely important.

As Ashley goes on to work and college, she'll inevitably be faced with stressful situations. But knowing that her art and family support are healthy resources, she'll be more likely to face stressors without substance use. Ashley's story might inspire you to think about what healthy activities you can turn to in tough times.

Resiliency Recap

It's not easy to talk about substance abuse. It's tempting to think it's not a big deal, and that it's a normal part of growing up. That is only partially true. We know that teens who don't regularly use alcohol, drugs, or tobacco are far more likely to be resilient when life gets tough.

If you haven't started, then don't start now. If you've already started, be honest with yourself. Are you using substances occasionally in social situations, or are you using them to cope with stressful feeling and situations? If you feel your substance use is impairing your ability to function in school or form relationships, you may need more help. Also, learning coping strategies that are fun and good for your body could pay off in a big way in a few months or years! And in the meantime, be nice to yourself. Remember to do something for yourself every single day.

PART II

Caring for Your Mental and Emotional Health

Engaging with the
world around you
every day

Caring for your
physical health

Resilience

Finding meaning,
joy, and purpose

Caring for your
mental and
emotional health

Mindfulness: Calming Your Mind and Body

Most of us spend a lot of time thinking about what happened to us in the past or what might happen in the future. In fact, at any given time, we are probably not really focused on what is happening right now. Of course, it's important to learn from the past and dream about the future, but it's also important to appreciate what's actually happening to you now—in the present moment.

The ability to be present also helps us fully enjoy what is happening to us. It promotes gratitude (in the good times) and helps us calm our anxieties (in more stressful times). The ability to be present and participate in the present moment is called *mindfulness*, and it's a key resilience skill. It can help you remember the good things that happen, and it can help you realize that stressful times don't last forever.

What Is Mindfulness?

Mindfulness is a resilience skill that can be learned and practiced in your everyday life.

---

mind·ful·ness (Oxford University Press 2020a)

1: The quality or state of being conscious or aware of something.

2: A mental state achieved by focusing one's awareness on the present moment, while acknowledging and accepting one's feelings, thoughts, and bodily sensations without judgment, used as a therapeutic technique.

The first definition basically means that you are paying attention to something. Are you aware of what is going on around—and inside of—you?

The second definition is the one we are going to use for the remainder of this book, because it defines mindfulness as an action. That makes it a skill. You can *practice* mindfulness by learning ways to focus your attention back to the present moment. So mindfulness isn't just a state of mind. It's not something that you are born with; it's something you can develop with patience and practice. You can use mindfulness almost anywhere—it doesn't require equipment or a special setting. But before we talk about how to practice mindfulness, let's talk about why it is such a powerful technique.

Why Be Mindful?

You might be wondering why you would want to pay attention to the world around you. Why would you want to pay attention to your thoughts and feelings? Sometimes, you might just feel like tuning everything out or distracting yourself from your problems. In fact, distraction isn't always a bad thing. Distraction works really well in the short term, but in the long term it might not work well if it is your only go-to strategy. Long term, you need to find ways to really deal with your feelings. Here are some key facts about the short-term and long-term benefits of mindfulness:

- Many studies suggest that mindfulness can help your attention and focus, and help you stay more organized (Mak et al. 2018).

- Mindfulness may help you cope when you are facing stressors, including chronic illness (Ahola Kohut et al. 2017).

Mindfulness is a useful resilience strategy because it helps you put the past and the future in perspective. Instead of getting carried away by your thoughts and feelings, mindfulness helps you learn to focus on how you can manage the present moment. There are many benefits of mindfulness, including better health and an overall feeling of calm. Let's look at Lauren and explore how mindfulness might benefit her as she plans for the future.

When Mindfulness Can Help: Lauren's Story

Lauren is a sixteen-year-old junior who is a great student. She is really worried about studying for her college entrance exams. She feels that if she doesn't get into a good college, she won't get a good job and she'll disappoint her family. Lauren's dad left when she was young, so she feels a lot of pressure to get a scholarship and make her family proud.

Lately, Lauren isn't sleeping well. Her thoughts race and sometimes she wakes up in middle of the night worried that she's going to fail an exam, miss a deadline, and just let everyone down. Sometimes, Lauren gets really bad headaches when she worries about the future.

Clearly, Lauren has a lot that she wants to achieve, and it's great that she wants to try to get a scholarship. Can you relate to that kind of drive? However, her intense focus on the future is interfering with her ability to sleep and is contributing to her headaches. It may be that when she becomes anxious, her fight-or-flight response is activated and her muscles tense up. She is thinking about all the things that might go wrong in the future, and her body is gearing up to deal with a lot of stress that isn't even happening yet. Lauren needs to find a way to bring herself back to the present moment, while still working toward her goals. This is where mindfulness skills can be useful.

Mindfulness is a basic way that we can get in touch with what is happening *right now*. The biggest benefits are that we pay more attention to things when they are good, and it stops us from getting overwhelmed when things aren't so great. If life throws a stressful situation your way, mindfulness skills can help you get through it.

To begin with, mindfulness can help you deal more effectively with all the thoughts in your head (check out You Are Not Your Thoughts, following). At any given time, we have many thoughts going through our head. We're always talking to ourselves. That's not crazy—it's human. If you add up all the thoughts that go through your head, you talk to yourself more than you talk to anyone else!

Do any of these thoughts sound familiar?

What a great game.

That guy is cute.

I hope I don't say something dumb.

I can't believe I failed that test.

This room is too noisy.

I'll never be able to learn this.

I wonder if I made the right decision.

What if I made a mistake?

When you start paying attention to the things you are saying to yourself, they are often about the past or the future. That's perfectly natural. But sometimes, we miss what is happening right in front of us because we're so focused on the past or the future. When you think about it, the only moment we can ever experience is this one. Right now, you are reading this sentence—not the one before, and not the one after. The past has already happened, and the future hasn't happened yet. You don't have to worry about whether you will understand the next sentence. You only have to appreciate that you just read this one. Sometimes, that can be a big relief, especially in times of stress.

In addition to helping you pay attention to your thoughts, mindfulness skills can help your body feel focused and more *grounded* in this moment. Grounding is similar to mindfulness because it means finding ways to connect with what is happening in your body and your surroundings, in the present moment.

In your teens, you might find that by paying attention to what is happening now, you are more likely to pay attention to the positive things you might be overlooking. Great athletes often describe a state of mindfulness during a tough game, when all they are doing is focusing on the current moment. Great writers and scientists talk about this feeling too—sometimes they get so focused on what they're doing that they forget about everything else—experiencing a sense of *flow*. Flow is similar to mindfulness, but it usually involves a single focus on a difficult goal or task.

Not only can mindfulness help you experience flow or feel grounded in the moment, but it also has benefits even if the present moment might be difficult. By facing your situation with a sense of calm and grounding, you are more likely to be able to think about your past mistakes and learn from them. When you learn from past mistakes, you can make better decisions for the future.

Resilient people are able to make good decisions. They also find ways to appreciate what they have in the moment. Mindfulness is a key resilience skill because it helps you focus on the present—life stressors may not feel as overwhelming when you deal with them one moment at a time, rather than all at once. These skills can also help you appreciate what is going well and not forget to pay attention to the good things.

Building Mindfulness into Your Life

There are so many ways you can bring your attention back to the present moment to help build resilience to deal with life's challenges. After you master the basics of mindful breathing (see below), you can explore techniques that involve your daily behaviors and hobbies, your thoughts, or your five senses to help you during times of stress. Try these different ways of practicing mindfulness and see what you enjoy.

Remember, mindfulness is also about nonjudgment, so be open to trying new things. And be kind to yourself until you find something that fits. Although mindfulness can help you feel calmer in the short term, it is also a long-term solution to helping you deal with stressful situations—making you more resilient.

THE BASIC ABDOMINAL BREATH

The first step in learning any mindfulness technique is to focus on the basics of breathing. Of course, you already know how to breathe, but mindful breathing means paying attention to the amazing way your body takes in air. Mindful breathing requires you to slow down a bit, making it easier to come back to the present moment. This kind of breathing helps you feel more calm and relaxed.

1. Start by putting one hand on your abdomen and one hand on your chest. Take a few normal breaths. You will probably feel your chest moving more than your abdomen.

2. Now take a few slower, deeper breaths. You will notice that your chest moves when you breathe, but try to get your abdomen to move as well. This is the way babies and dogs breathe—through their "belly."

3. Slowly count to 10, and with each breath, try to get air from your nose and mouth, through your chest, and all the way down to your abdomen. Feel the air flow all the way in and all the way out.

4. When you feel yourself getting distracted (and it's very likely you will feel distracted), gently bring your attention back to your breath. You can repeat the word "breathe" or you can count each breath ("1… 2… 3…"). The important thing is to gently bring your attention back to your breathing whenever you feel your thoughts wandering into the past and future. As you breathe, notice how you feel. Do you start to feel your muscles relax a bit? Do your thoughts slow down just a little? Do you feel less worried?

5. If you find yourself becoming *more* worried after doing deep breathing, go easy on yourself. If you are used to being worried, it might actually feel strange to "let go." If you are having trouble with this kind of breathing, start by doing it in an environment where you feel really calm and safe, or maybe ask someone you trust to try it with you.

6. See if you can practice this kind of breathing for 30 breaths every day. You can do it anywhere, though it's easiest to start by practicing in a quiet, calm

space. Eventually, you can challenge yourself to "breathe into your abdomen" in all sorts of settings—while sitting in class, hanging out with your friends, or listening to music. No one will notice—except you!

Now that you've learned about the basics of breathing, you're ready to see how other mindfulness techniques might fit into your life. The breath is the base of all mindfulness exercises, and now we'll focus on how to build on it. Once you start paying attention to your breath, try to see how other activities can help you focus on the present moment.

Learning mindfulness doesn't mean becoming a monk. There are so many things you do in your everyday life that can help bring you back to the present moment, which will help you better handle stress. In all these activities, remember to focus on your breathing. It's also normal and expected if you sometimes experience difficult feelings during these exercises: worry, sadness, disappointment, frustration. The key is to let those emotions exist alongside what you are doing now, and try to focus on the present.

There is no right or wrong way to practice these exercises. The important thing is for you to be able to use these skills in stressful times. And to do this, it's helpful if they're part of your routine most of the time. Try to find one or two activities that allow you to connect yourself to the present moment: walking, art making, chores, eating, prayer, or any activity that works for you. Try to do one of these activities every day, even if it's just for a few minutes. Here are some suggestions to try.

MINDFULNESS AND MOVEMENT

Mindfulness can involve physical activities you do every day. This way, you don't have to go out of your way to create a special mindfulness routine.

- **Mindful walk.** When you walk to school or to a friend's house, pay attention to each step. Notice your feet making contact with the ground. Pay attention to your body posture. Is it straight or is your back hunched over? Notice the feel of the air on your face. Pay attention to the sounds around you. Do you hear the rustling of the leaves? Or is the sun hot on the concrete and your skin? As your thoughts wander, gently bring them back to the present, to the feel of your shoes on the ground and the sights and sounds in the air.

- **Mindful chores.** The next time you are doing chores around the house (for example, washing dishes or doing the laundry), try not to distract yourself. Instead, really pay attention to what you're doing and to the sights, sounds, smells, and textures around you. Use all of your senses. If you're doing dishes, feel the warm soapy water on your hands. Feel the soft sponge. If you're doing laundry, take a minute to pay attention to which clothes feel softer and which feel more textured. Notice the smell of the soap and the sights and sounds around you. Maybe it's the feel of metal spoons as you wash the dishes. Perhaps it is the cold metal of the clothes dryer on your fingers. Rather than thinking about what you will do after the task is finished, repeat to yourself, *This is what I am doing now, in this moment.* Continue to breathe as you immerse yourself in what you are doing.

You can use this approach to any physical activity you are doing. Just slow down and pay attention to the movement and sensations you are feeling. You can use a similar approach by really learning to focus on something you enjoy.

MINDFUL HOBBIES

Here are two ways to practice mindfulness with things you do in your free time. If you can build mindfulness into things you already enjoy, it'll become a habit.

- **Mindful art.** If you enjoy art, draw or paint a picture. As you decide what to create, pay attention to the movement of your hands. Appreciate how your hands are able to bring what you're thinking to life on the page. Pay attention to the colors you're selecting. As you breathe, continue to appreciate that you're doing something you enjoy in this moment. If you find yourself having thoughts about the past or worries about the future, simply focus again on your hands, the colors you have chosen, and your breath.

- **Mindful singing.** The next time you sing along to a song you love, pay attention to the words. Focus on how you feel. Notice your facial muscles. Are you smiling? Is your body moving to the beat? Just enjoy the present moment—being fully immersed in the music you enjoy.

You can apply this kind of practice to any activity you enjoy.

MINDFUL EATING

Here are two more activities that you do every day: eating and drinking. See what it feels like to bring mindfulness to your next meal.

- **Mindful meals.** The next time you eat a meal, try to do so without any distractions. Put away your electronics and turn off any music. Before you start eating, take a minute to think about where your food comes from. Think about the farm where the wheat or vegetables grew. Think about the truck driver who had to bring the raw ingredients to a factory and the journey that all of the raw ingredients had to take—how many hands the ingredients had to pass though before reaching your plate in this form. Take a moment to be grateful to all of the people who are making this moment, this meal, possible for you. Think about the smell of your food.

    When you are ready, start to eat. When you do so, really pay attention to how the food tastes. Is it salty or sweet? Does the taste linger? Are you eating quickly or savoring your bites? Continue to eat and breathe, really focusing on your food and the experience of eating.

If you enjoy this kind of exercise, try it every day with something very simple, like an apple, an orange, or even a cold glass of milk. You can make a mindful snack a part of your routine.

- **Mindful water.** The next time you take a sip of water, pay attention to how your mouth and taste buds feel before you take a drink. Once the water is in your mouth, just notice the temperature. As you swallow the water, think of it moving down your esophagus in slow motion. Really pay attention to your body sensations. It can be quite amazing to appreciate all the body parts that work together to take a sip of water.

You might be noticing that mindfulness can apply to many situations, from your everyday activities like eating and walking to things you enjoy. What else can you try mindfulness with?

MINDFUL SPIRITUAL PRACTICE

Of course, mindfulness can also apply to times when you are more focused on meditation or concentration. This is a great time to see whether this kind of mindfulness practice is for you!

- **Mindful meditation or prayer.** If you are someone who comes from a religious or spiritual background, you may want to try daily prayer or meditation. Pick a time every day to take a few breaths and think about what you are grateful for. Think about what you believe, and ask for the blessings you wish for yourself, your family, and your friends. Take a moment and feel a connection with something or someone greater. Allow your worries to be carried by a force outside of you. Notice your breath and your thoughts as you focus on the present moment.

- **Mindful gratitude.** At the same time every day, take a minute to appreciate something positive that is happening right now. It can be simple, like being grateful for a moment to sit down and take a break. Maybe you are grateful for the sun that is shining, or the pretty-looking snow you see.

> Just take a moment to notice the positive things that are happening, even if they seem small or unimportant.

These kinds of activities are a strong foundation for resilience—the ability to bounce back from setbacks and deal with stress. Mindfulness activities can help you appreciate positive experiences as they're happening, and they can help refocus your thoughts if you're getting lost in past or future worries.

Mindfulness to Deal with Difficult Feelings

As I noted before, we are always talking to ourselves—you talk with yourself more than you talk to anyone else! Our thoughts have a natural impact on how we're feeling. For example, if you're thinking, *I can't believe I didn't make the team,* you are likely to feel sad or disappointed. If you think, *I'm pretty sure my audition isn't going to go well,* you may experience feelings of anxiety. Or some of those thoughts might lead to more difficult feelings. Although the next skill deals more with this issue, a mindfulness practice can help you get some perspective on painful thoughts *and* feelings. With practice, you don't have to get caught up in the specific details of your thoughts and feelings, especially if they are about the past or the future. You can just learn to observe them and allow them to pass by.

The next time you are feeling nervous or upset about something, try to get some distance from your own thoughts using some mindfulness skills. Usually, thoughts that make us the most upset are about the past or the future. This skill is somewhere in between *attacking* your worries and *accepting* them. It's about allowing your worries to exist but also about getting a little space in between you and your thoughts.

There are many kinds of visualizations that might help you practice this skill. Let's look at a few of them now.

YOU ARE NOT YOUR THOUGHTS

Set a timer and try each of these visualizations for one to two minutes, and see which ones work for you. Once you find something you like, you can try it a few times a week, especially when you are upset about something.

When you practice these techniques, be sure to pay attention to your body. Try to feel your feet on the floor, and pay attention to how you are sitting and the flow of your breath. This will help you stay focused on the present moment.

- **Picture yourself on a soft, fluffy cloud.** You are secure, comfortable, and supported. You can see your thoughts floating by on other clouds that pass you by. You realize that you are not your thoughts, because you are still sitting securely on your own cloud. Some of your thoughts are difficult, and they pass by on dark and stormy-looking clouds. Other thoughts are more pleasant, and they float away slowly. As you breathe, picture the clouds passing you one by one. You can label the difficult thoughts as "storm clouds" and the more neutral or positive thoughts as "fluffy clouds." Whatever the label, remember that you are not jumping onto any of the clouds. You just watch them pass by.

- **Picture a long freight train.** There are many, many cars on this train. And your thoughts are the passengers. You're just watching the cars of the train pass by with all of your thoughts. Some thoughts are in cars labeled "difficult" and some thoughts are in cars labeled "pleasant." Maybe some thoughts are labeled "to-do list" or "worries." Some thoughts roll by in unlabeled cars, and that's fine too. Just practice watching them roll by, because you know you don't have to hop on the train.

- **Picture yourself in a baggage claim.** Many suitcases go by, all full of your thoughts. Some suitcases are big and heavy. Others looks very nice and neat. Every now and then a box goes by. You don't need to pick up any of the suitcases. You are free to just watch your thoughts pass by on the baggage claim, while your feet are firmly planted on the ground.

- **Picture a long, beautiful stream.** You can see your thoughts floating by on it. Some of your thoughts are on beautiful leaves that have just fallen. These thoughts go by effortlessly. Other thoughts come down on big tree branches. Sometimes, these larger branches start to get stuck and want to dig into the shore, but the pressure of the water keeps them moving along eventually. You see flowers, sticks, and leaves of all shapes and sizes coming down the stream, all carrying your thoughts. And as you sit on the shore, you are able to appreciate everything that passes by.

Learning to *observe your thoughts* without getting overly involved in their content is challenging, but it can help you deal with difficult feelings like anxiety or sadness.

In addition, some specific grounding techniques can help you when you feel upset or worried. As I mentioned above, grounding can help you connect with what is happening in your body and in your surroundings in the present moment. So let's move on from thoughts and feelings, and explore how mindfulness skills can help you get grounded in your body and senses. This can help you learn healthy ways to deal with stress in the moment—which is an important part of resilience.

GROUNDING SKILLS

Grounding techniques are ways that you can focus on the present moment, particularly during times of stress. They usually involve using your body and senses to bring your attention to what is going on right now. The next time you are upset, angry, or anxious, here are some things you can try:

- **Use your sense of smell.** Choose a candle or a scent that you find pleasant, then take a few deep breaths. Try to focus on being in the present moment, fully experiencing the scent in the room. If your thoughts wander, gently bring them back to the present moment.

- **Use your sense of touch.** Maybe you have a favorite blanket or a stress ball. Pay attention to what your favorite object feels like in your hands. Is it rough or smooth? Is it cold or warm? Touch can be a very powerful mindfulness tool that helps you center yourself when you feel overwhelmed.

- **Use your sense of taste.** Pour yourself a glass of cold water or juice with ice. As you drink, pay attention to your sensations. If you find your thoughts wandering, bring yourself back to how your body is feeling. Pay attention to how your taste buds are responding. Take a few breaths in between each sip and gently focus on this moment.

- **Use your sense of hearing.** Choose a piece of music that you love and allow yourself to listen to it with no distractions. Sit down and listen to the notes of the melody without talking to anyone else. Just give yourself a few minutes to listen and enjoy the music. If you feel yourself going back to what is bothering you, tell yourself you will get back to it in three minutes, when your song is over. For now, allow yourself to be fully immersed in the music.

- **Use your sense of sight.** Look at your favorite piece of art, your favorite picture, or at something outside—like trees, snow, a rough stone, or blades of grass. Pay attention to the colors and shapes you see. Notice all the details. As you shift your eyes, notice the light around you. Is it bright or dim? Are there shadows? Take a minute and breathe, allowing yourself to really see what is front of you.

Finding the Right Mindful Practice: Lauren's Journey Continues

Earlier, we talked about Lauren. She was worried about her future, having difficulty sleeping, and didn't want to let her family down. Lauren decided to experiment with various mindfulness techniques and found that she really enjoyed taking a short walk every day.

During her walk, she took time to notice the color of the trees and the sounds of dogs in the park. At first, Lauren felt like she was wasting time, but she told herself that for ten minutes a day it was okay to do nothing.

After a few weeks, Lauren began to feel calmer, and although she still experienced headaches, she found that they were less frequent. She also found that when her mind began to wander to the future, she was able to come back to the moment by washing her face with cool water and taking a few deep breaths. By focusing on the present, Lauren found that her sleep also began to improve.

Resiliency Recap

Mindfulness does not take away your problems or challenges. But it can help you deal with the rush of thoughts in your head. It can help you create a sense of calm, focus, and grounding that is beneficial in many situations, such as when you're studying for a difficult test, relaxing before bed, learning to tune out distractions, or truly enjoying hanging out with your friends.

Mindfulness can be used every day to build up your resilience, and it can also be used in the moment to help you tolerate difficult feelings, helping you deal with stress more effectively. Other skills in this book will discuss how talking to others can help you deal with stress, but mindfulness is one great way to learn to appreciate the positive aspects in your life and become more focused on what you're doing.

Tolerating Difficult Emotions Without Becoming Overwhelmed

When we study people who are resilient in times of stress, one of the key things we notice is that they have the ability to deal with strong feelings and emotions. Sometimes, we make the mistake of thinking that resilient people don't actually experience strong emotions—that they have somehow learned to be calm at all times. That's not true at all. Instead, they can identify, deal with, and express what they are feeling in safe spaces. Psychologists say that they have a high level of *distress tolerance*, meaning that they can tolerate difficult feelings, thoughts, and sensations well—and bounce back from them. Another term for this is *emotional tolerance* (Linehan 1993).

---

e·mo·tion·al tol·er·ance (Linehan 1993)

1: The ability to endure difficult emotions or physical sensations.

2: Skills required to manage stressful emotions during times of stress and adversity.

You'll learn all about emotional tolerance skills in this section. But first, let's consider what messages you may have received about strong feelings.

Why Is Emotional Tolerance Important?

When you are upset, have you heard the following from friends, family, or other well-meaning people in your life?

Don't cry. It will be okay.

Don't get upset. This isn't the worst thing.

You can handle this. Stop worrying.

You need to _____ [breathe, do exercise, forget about this].

Don't overreact.

You just need to get your mind off things.

You are taking this too seriously.

You need to stay strong.

Chances are, you've heard the statements above a lot. Maybe you've said them to yourself. Maybe you've said them to other people. We live in a culture that doesn't like strong emotions. We deal with unwanted feelings by trying to get them to go away as soon as possible. This makes sense in the short term—we can outrun strong feelings and emotions for a while. But in the long term, this approach doesn't work. Maybe you have found yourself avoiding stressful situations and emotions only to feel your emotions come back stronger than ever. Let's see how Dave handles his strong feelings in social situations.

Socially Awkward: Dave's Story

Dave is a fifteen-year-old freshman in high school. He is a good student but doesn't have a lot of friends. He tends to get nervous in new groups, so he avoids joining clubs or sports. He worries about saying the wrong thing and wonders if other people will find him boring. Whenever he is around other kids—waiting for the bus or for class to start—Dave avoids eye contact with others. He usually looks down at his phone and plays a game. The kids usually leave Dave alone.

You can see that Dave's use of his cell phone to distract himself from uncomfortable social situations works well in the short term. Can you relate to Dave's social anxiety? If so, you probably make the connection that if you don't attract the attention of people around you, you can reduce your anxiety in the toughest moments. However, this strategy actually increases Dave's anxiety in the long term. How? Because the more Dave avoids any kind of contact, the more he's likely to believe that he has nothing interesting to say. He never gets any practice talking to new people, so he continues to avoid them and social situations. It's an anxiety cycle that can last a long time!

Obviously, this isn't going to be a strategy that Dave—or you—can use forever. If he gets a summer job, he will have to talk to new people. If he takes college classes, he will have to interact with people he doesn't know. In the long term, if Dave never learns to deal with his anxiety, it's unlikely that he'll be able to make new friends or try new things. Basically, every time he avoids his problems, he makes it harder to break his pattern of avoidance.

Resilient people know that it's okay to feel strong emotions. They've worked on ways to let themselves experience those emotions without becoming overwhelmed. Sadly, our culture confuses being strong with being stoic—which means not showing emotion at all. Sometimes we avoid our emotions so often that they become overwhelming later on.

For example, maybe you try to avoid expressing small amounts of anger, only to have a big outburst later. Emotional outbursts that you feel you can't control (for instance, uncontrollable crying, yelling, or fear) may be the result of avoiding negative feelings as they build up. Basically, it's like ignoring the first few drops of rain; before you know it, you're caught in a thunderstorm.

When we look at people who are resilient, we see that they have learned how to experience their emotions, not push them away. With practice, their emotional muscles are well developed—meaning they can tolerate strong, heavy emotions. Here are some key facts we know about distress tolerance, or the ability to handle tough feelings:

- Learning distress tolerance may protect you from developing depression during times of stress (Felton et al. 2019).

- Teens with higher distress tolerance levels are less likely to smoke cigarettes regularly (Shadur et al. 2017), which may help you be physically healthier in the future.

- Learning to better manage difficult emotions can make you a safer driver (Scott-Parker 2017) and less likely to be involved in a car accident.

Developing Emotional Tolerance

The good news is that emotional tolerance, like all the other skills is this book, is something that can be learned and practiced. *Emotions* are often longer-lasting states that influenced the development of our physiology as human beings. Emotions are hardwired into our bodies, and we've been experiencing the same kinds of basic emotions since we were cavemen! For example, everyone experiences *basic emotions* like *happiness, sadness, anger,* and *fear.* Our brain and body actually secrete certain chemicals and hormones when we are in these states (Ekman 1984).

Feelings are usually shorter-term states that come and go. *Feelings* are usually one word and can be used to describe your deeper emotion—or what you are experiencing inside. The first step in learning to tolerate *emotions* is to identify what you are feeling. Here are examples of feelings:

- Joy
- Satisfaction
- Pride
- Gratitude
- Enthusiasm
- Excitement
- Motivation
- Determination
- Irritation

- Rejection
- Hopelessness
- Loneliness
- Nervousness
- Confusion
- Insecurity
- Distraction
- Disappointment
- Frustration

IDENTIFY YOUR FEELINGS

A big step you can take in tolerating strong emotions that may be longer lasting is to learn to identify what you are feeling in the moment. Set a repeating alarm on your phone every morning, afternoon, and evening at times that are convenient for you (that is, not during biology class). When you hear the alarm, challenge yourself to come up with at least three words to describe how you are feeling. You can write them down in a note on your phone, text them to yourself, or just say them aloud to yourself. Keep in mind that feelings are usually just one word.

You don't have to make any effort to change what you are feeling. This is just about checking in with yourself more often. If you choose to write down your feelings, over time, you'll be able to look back and see whether any patterns emerge. Maybe you feel nervous in the morning because your math class is first period. Or relieved in the evening because you get to practice basketball.

Primary Emotions and Secondary Feelings

Once you start to identify your emotions, you can also start to observe how primary emotions and secondary feelings are different from each other. The first thing you experience is usually called your *primary emotion*. Remember that emotions are usually basic experiences like sadness, happiness, fear, or anger—and your body often has a physical reaction to them (like crying, smiling, sweating, or heart racing). Your *secondary feeling* is what you feel in response to that emotion. For example, you might feel *ashamed* that you are *sad* or *depressed*, or you might become *irritated* that you are *fearful* or *anxious*. You are already feeling *sad* or *fearful* (primary emotions).

But you make your primary emotions worse when you beat yourself up for feeling them. For example, when we try to run away from or avoid feelings of sadness, the result is that we experience additional painful feelings, including anxiety or anger.

Sometimes you might feel overwhelmed from experiencing many negative feelings at the same time. It might help to try to think about what your main emotion is. It's like peeling back the layers of an onion. Ask yourself, *Is there something behind this?* For example, maybe you're feeling angry at a friend, but when you look at what's behind that anger, you realize that you feel hurt and sad that you were left out of a party. Or maybe you feel frustrated that your parents are so strict, but when you look behind the frustration, you see that you're really worried that your friends won't like you if you can't hang out all the time.

As you keep peeling back the layers of the onion, you might actually find that all the *feelings* lead to a more basic, core *emotion*—like happiness, sadness, anger, or fear. Identifying your secondary feelings is helpful—particularly if your secondary feelings are causing you more stress or suffering. Learning to allow your primary emotion, while letting the secondary feeling go, is a very useful skill during tough times.

IDENTIFY EMOTIONS AND SECONDARY FEELINGS

The next time you are in a stressful situation, try to see whether you can identify your primary emotions and secondary feelings. Primary emotions are usually simple, and you might even feel them in your body. For example, your heart is racing because you are worried; you have a lump in your throat because you feel sad; you are sweating more because you are angry. Secondary feelings often have to do with judgments we make about ourselves. Sometimes these judgments can add to our suffering.

When you're in a situation that involves a difficult emotion, identify what you're saying to yourself and how you're feeling. Then see whether you have secondary messages to yourself. See whether your secondary feelings are making you feel worse. This takes practice, so don't be discouraged if it takes you a while to think about situations in this way. Some examples:

Message to Yourself	Primary Emotion	Secondary Message to Yourself	Secondary Feeling
I should have studied more for this test.	Anxiety	You are an idiot for not studying more.	Shame
I'm so upset my boyfriend broke up with me.	Sadness	Everyone is going to be talking about this.	Embarrassment
I can't believe the teacher accused me of cheating when I didn't.	Anger	Other people would have spoken up for themselves.	Disappointment (directed at myself)
I can't believe I got the lead in the play.	Happiness	I bet I'm not really good enough for this.	Self-doubt

Painful or difficult emotions also don't last forever. Earlier, we talked about Dave and his avoidance of feeling anxious. Let's continue his story to find out what he discovered.

Identifying Primary Emotions: Dave Challenges Himself

With some practice, Dave is able to understand that the primary emotion he's feeling in social situations is fear and anxiety. He's able to identify that he feels unworthy and boring because he's unable to make new friends.

Dave decides to allow himself to feel his anxiety the next time he's waiting outside of school by not immediately taking refuge in his cell phone. For the next week, he doesn't look at his phone while he is waiting to go to class. Instead, he practices deep breathing and allows himself to make eye contact with people. Dave notices that his anxiety usually reaches its peak when he is first waiting outside of school. He also notices that after a few minutes, his anxiety level begins to go down on its own.

On the fourth day of this, a classmate approaches Dave and says, "You're in my math class, right? Do you know what we were supposed to do for homework?" Dave is able to face his strong emotions and is on his way to becoming more confident in social situations.

When we stop avoiding difficult thoughts and feelings, we can pay attention to what is happening around us and to our primary emotions. In the present moment, we may find that there are actually positive things happening that we aren't noticing. We may also find that the uncomfortable thoughts and feelings don't last as long as we thought they would.

Most of the time, avoiding difficult thoughts and feelings actually makes things worse. Thoughts and feelings are like text messages—they have a way of pinging until they get noticed. Think of it this way: when you have a text message, you may see constant reminders pop up until you acknowledge that you've seen it by swiping over the alert.

SEE HOW LONG YOUR EMOTIONS LAST

In skill 3 you learned how to deal with strong, difficult feelings using different mindfulness strategies. Here are a few things to try that combine mindfulness with building up your emotional tolerance:

- **Get a little distance from your emotions.** Sometimes it can be helpful to put space between you and your emotion. So the next time you are feeling a strong positive or negative emotion, try to imagine that the feeling is in a box on a conveyor belt. Each box is clearly labeled with the feeling you are experiencing. You are standing on the side, watching your emotion go by. Don't make any effort to change what you're feeling. Just observe it.

    Count out loud to find out how long you can see each box. When the box is out of view, it means the emotion is fading away. Ask yourself whether the emotion lasted as long as you thought it would.

- **Raise your hand when you are feeling an intense feeling.** Yes, this might sound a bit silly, but it's actually a very good demonstration of how your feelings may *seem* like they last forever but they actually don't. So give it a try. (And you can do it when you're alone, so you don't embarrass yourself.) Rate the intensity of your feeling on a scale of 1 to 5. For example, a rating of 1 might be "I am a bit disappointed" to 5 being "I feel absolutely disappointed." Keep your hand raised, and as you feel the intensity of your emotion going down, lower your hand more and more, until your hand is back at your side. Notice that your emotion doesn't stay at a high level of intensity forever.

Expressing Your Feelings

Another aspect of developing your emotional muscles and strengthening emotional tolerance is learning how to *express your strong feelings appropriately*, without ignoring them or letting them build up to the point of an uncontrollable outburst of crying or yelling. Once you allow yourself to feel things, you need safe places to express your feelings. At times, you may find yourself trying to numb your emotions instead of actually feeling them, because you are afraid of getting hurt or feeling vulnerable. Or you may find yourself trying to "stuff" your emotions down. Can you see yourself in any of these statements?

I'm better off forgetting about this.

I'm not going to tell them how I feel.

I'm not going to let myself get sad about this.

It's not worth talking about.

No one cares about me anyway.

I'm being ungrateful if I express anything negative.

If you feel like some of these statements apply to you, you might benefit from learning to express emotions that make you feel vulnerable. Not only is it normal to have negative and difficult emotions, but it's also normal to want to express those emotions in healthy ways. Expressing your emotions doesn't mean you'll make them worse, and it doesn't mean you're being ungrateful. In fact, you may even find that tough emotions lose a little bit of their control over you once they are expressed.

EXPRESS YOURSELF

It can be really scary to allow yourself to express difficult emotions. However, you might discover that once you label what you're feeling and say the words aloud, the emotion actually loses some of its power.

The next time you're feeling something very intense—like anger, sadness, disappointment, or anxiety—instead of numbing or stuffing the feelings until you have an outburst you can't control, try these suggestions. First, rate your emotion on a scale of 1 (not intense) to 10 (very intense). Then see whether any of these techniques help you tolerate and eventually reduce the intensity of your emotions:

- **Write down what you are feeling.** For example, "I'm feeling really help-less right now." Then add, "But this won't last forever." Write those sentences ten times. Or text it to yourself. But you can't copy and paste—the trick is that you need to actually write it out ten times and see whether the emotion loses some of its intensity. Each time you read the statement, ask yourself, *Am I still feeling this emotion with the same intensity?*

- **Look in the mirror and talk to yourself.** Yes, you will definitely feel silly. Start with stating what you're feeling, for example, "I'm hurt and worried that no one will care." Then ask yourself, *Am I really 100 percent sure of this feeling?* Take a deep breath. Now do this ten more times and see whether you still feel as intensely.

- **Tell someone how you're feeling.** This is a difficult one, but try to choose someone you love and trust, if you can. Tell them, "I'm not looking for advice, I just want to vent. I'm really feeling _____ [sad, frustrated, upset, angry, hurt, or whatever you're feeling]." Try to do this at least once a week to really build your emotional tolerance muscles. Skill 7 talks a lot more about social support, so that section will help you if you are having trouble thinking about who to choose.

Resiliency Recap

We need to change our old ideas. Being stoic or unemotional isn't the same as being strong. The truth is that everyone experiences strong emotions. Stressful times come with strong emotions, and that's okay. What makes you emotionally resilient is having the courage to feel your feelings instead of avoiding them or letting them build up until they feel overwhelming.

There are many ways you can build up your tolerance for strong emotions, including identifying your primary emotions, letting go of secondary feelings that add to your stress, using mindfulness to see how long difficult emotions actually last (it's often not as long as you may think), and learning to give voice to your emotions—on paper, in the mirror, or to someone else.

Emotional tolerance takes practice and patience, but with time you'll find yourself becoming more confident that you can deal with strong emotions and challenging times. You might even find that you become a role model for your friends and family.

Learning from the Past by Transforming Shame

When we look at resilient people, one thing becomes clear: they have all experienced setbacks or obstacles, and they use these difficult circumstances as opportunities to change and grow. Think about your own life. Sometimes the obstacles you experience aren't anyone's fault. For example, maybe your family had to move across the country and you had to learn to make friends at a new school. Maybe you had to learn online for a while, because your school was dealing with ongoing health risks.

Some obstacles can have a profound impact on your life. For example, maybe your parents got a divorce, and you had to learn to adjust to splitting time between two homes. Maybe you had to figure out how to deal with parents who aren't communicating well with each other. In some situations, you clearly aren't at fault because the adults in your life made decisions that affected you, and you didn't get a say in how to handle things.

There may also be times when you feel like you did something to contribute to a setback. For example, maybe you didn't do your homework or study for math most of the semester, and now you're facing a pretty bad grade. Perhaps you repeated nasty rumors about a friend, and now you are dealing with some hurt feelings in your friend group.

Typically, our first reaction when we've done something wrong is to shut down or become defensive. But resilient people use these situations as an opportunity for growth. This section focuses on the situations when you might have done something to contribute to a stressful situation or setback—and how to learn from these occasions too.

A key to resilience is looking at setbacks or obstacles and figuring out:

1. What was in my control?

2. What can I learn from the situation?

3. What can I forgive myself for?

Two terms will help us as we explore these questions: *shame* and *guilt*.

---

shame (Oxford University Press 2020c)

1: A painful feeling of humiliation or distress caused by the consciousness of wrong or foolish behavior.

2: A condition of humiliating disgrace or disrepute.

In psychology, we tend to think of shame as a feeling that reflects on you as a person. For example, you might feel shame and think you are a bad person when you hurt someone's feelings, take something that doesn't belong to you, or lie to get what you want. When you experience shame, you react to a situation by feeling you are damaged and inadequate as a person. You might think, *I'm a horrible person. I deserved this.*

Guilt is related to shame, but it is also different in several important ways.

guilt (Merriam-Webster 2020e)

1: The fact of having committed a breach of conduct.

2: The state of one who has committed an offense especially consciously.

3: A feeling of deserving blame for offenses.

In the same situation, one individual might experience shame and another might experience guilt. When we react with *guilt*, we focus on how we handled a situation; when we react with *shame*, we focus on our traits—how we perceive ourselves as a whole. For example, maybe you are tired and say something mean to a friend who needs to talk. If you feel shame, you think about what a bad person you are for not being supportive. If you feel guilt, you tell yourself you need to apologize to your friend and make sure you listen next time, even if you feel tired.

From a psychological perspective, most people find it easier to experience guilt because it is "controllable." Unlike shame, guilt can actually help you learn from mistakes. Guilt helps you take responsibility for your actions—though it's not a way of getting yourself off the hook for things you regret. If you did something mean in a specific situation—and you feel bad about it—you can learn from it and make different choices in the future.

The person who is experiencing guilt is more likely to use healthy coping, and the person who experiences shame is more likely to feel stuck (Shen 2018). With shame, you might feel like you are just a bad or terrible person. That doesn't give you much motivation to change! The figures below will help you understand the difference between guilt and shame.

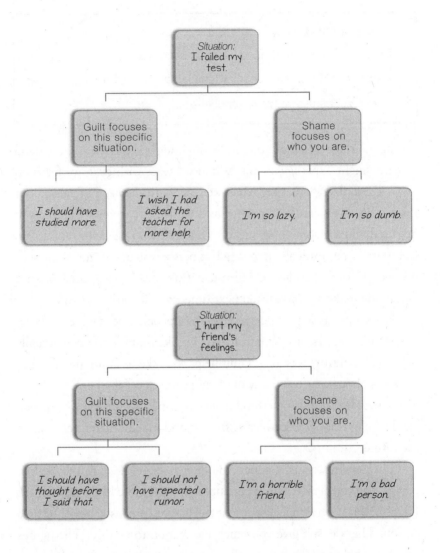

When you feel shame, you are much more likely to make the same mistakes over and over again, because you think that's just who you are. If you feel guilt, you can actually change your behavior. This section will help you look at prior setbacks and future obstacles, and how to turn shame into guilt. That means figuring out what you *can* control, learning from your mistakes, and forgiving yourself for things you might have done differently. The benefits include having better relationships with other people, having more self-respect, and feeling more optimistic about the future.

Caution: Societal Prejudice Is Never Your Fault

It's important to note that stigmatizing messages from others, including parents and other adults, can also influence our feelings of shame. It can be really difficult to let go of shame if you are being told that you're a bad person by the people around you, especially if it is about something you cannot change. In that case, your shame is the result of prejudice or stigma—not because of anything you've done wrong!

Here are some key facts to know about shame:

- Shame can be associated with your sexual orientation or gender identity.

- Shame can be associated with your race, ethnicity, or religion.

- If you are a survivor of abuse—particularly sexual abuse—you might feel shame.

- Shame can be associated with your weight or other body dissatisfaction.

- Shame can increase your risk of mental health problems, including depression (Tilghman-Osborne et al. 2008).

I cannot say this enough. No one should be shamed for who they are. No one should be made to feel inferior for their gender identify, sexual orientation, race or ethnicity, religion, trauma history, or appearance. Maybe people may have tried to shame you when you spoke up about experiences of discrimination, violence, or abuse. These are not things you need to change about yourself. The world needs to change—and the people who are saying unkind things and treating people as inferior need to change! If you are struggling with these issues and need more support, the Resources section of this book has more information for you. This section is focused on the difference between guilt and shame when you've actually done something you *want* to change.

What Is the Purpose of Shame?

You might be wondering why we feel difficult emotions like shame. Well, it helps to understand why we feel difficult sensations at all. Let's take the example of pain. If you accidentally touch something very hot, your body releases chemicals to signal to your brain that you're in pain. The feeling of pain is overwhelming, and you immediately remove your hand from the heat. This protects your body from tissue damage.

Similarly, shame involves intense reactions in your mind and body. The purpose of these strong sensations is to protect your relationships and social bonds (Breggin 2015). For example, if you steal someone's lunch and you later see them experiencing hunger, you might feel shame—like you are a bad person across the board. If you push someone out of the way to get to the front of the line, you might feel shame—like you are a bully.

The evolutionary purpose of shame is to get us to cooperate with each other, to work well in groups. Think of it from the perspective of the caveman. The emotion of shame helped people in the same community cooperate with each other. After all, shame keeps us from stealing each other's stuff and hurting other people. That is a good thing.

The problem with shame is that it often becomes a generalized feeling. *Guilt* is usually about a situation, but *shame* is about who you are as a person. When you experience too much shame, you might feel overwhelmed and unsure of whether you can ever do better, so you might keep continuing an unhealthy behavior, because you feel powerless to change it. And if you give up trying to change, you can never learn from your own experiences. Let's look at Brian's story.

Shame Can Keep You Stuck: Brian's Story

Brian is a fourteen-year-old freshman whose parents recently got a divorce. Brian and his sister move into an apartment with their mom, and they both have to attend a new high school. Because playing on the basketball team is one of his major accomplishments, Brian is really disappointed when he doesn't make the team at his new school. Brian misses his old friends and teachers but never talks to anyone about it. Instead, he gets more and more angry that he was forced to move.

He starts stealing things from a local store and cheating on tests. After he does these things, Brian feels awful. He tells himself that he's "a failure" and that "nothing matters anyway." Basically, Brian feels powerless to change his behavior because he has labeled himself a failure, meaning he can never improve or do anything differently.

When we look at Brian's story, we see a lot of shame because he has labeled his entire character (*a failure*) as opposed to his choices (*I'm not doing the right things by cheating and taking stuff*). Of course, it's not good that Brian is stealing things or cheating on tests. But you can see that by calling himself a failure, there's no motivation to change—instead, it keeps him stuck in a cycle of unhealthy behavior. This is why it's important to learn to transform shame into guilt. For example, if Brian had told himself, *I feel really bad about what I'm doing. This isn't who I am,* he might have been able to figure out how to do things differently. For instance, maybe he would have decided to talk to someone about how he was feeling or figure out whether he could join another sport.

Guilt has more to do with a situation and less to do with your whole personality or who you are. With guilt, you don't broadly decide that you are a bad person; you just recognize that you did something that wasn't right. Guilt doesn't get you off the hook, though. You still have to figure out what you can change and try to do better, but it doesn't define who you are in the way that shame does.

Let's get back to Brian's example. What if, instead of beating himself up over the shoplifting and cheating, Brian was able to learn from it? That's actually what happened when he eventually got caught stealing chips from the local store. Luckily, because it was his first offense, the store owner decided to call just his mom.

When Brian talked to his mom, he admitted he had been stealing and cheating on tests, and he told her how bad he felt after moving. They discussed how not making the basketball team was such a disappointment. Although Brian's mom couldn't fix the situation, she did arrange for him to go to his old neighborhood twice a week and play basketball with his friends.

After a few months, Brian began to make some friends at his new school. He still missed his old neighborhood, but he was happy he was still hanging out with his old friends. And instead of thinking of his shoplifting and cheating with shame, he began to take the responsibility associated with guilt. He told his mom, "I definitely didn't deal with the whole move very well. But I guess I didn't realize how hard it was going to be. I know I'm not making those mistakes again."

Remember that *shame* has to do with how you judge yourself as person, while *guilt* has to do with how you handled a situation. Here are some clues to help you decode shame versus guilt thoughts.

Examples of shame thoughts:	**Examples of guilt thoughts:**
I'm a loser.	*I shouldn't have done that.*
I'm dumb.	*I wish I didn't say that.*
I'm mean.	*I have to figure out how to do better.*
I'm lazy.	*I feel bad about how I acted.*
I'll never be as good as my friends.	*I should have known better.*
There's nothing decent about me.	
I just do stupid things.	

CATCH THE SHAME AND DESCRIBE IT

It's normal to have times when you feel disappointed or upset with yourself. Maybe you didn't do well on a test, you were mean to your little sister, or you forgot someone's birthday. The next time you are feeling bad about yourself, write down exactly what you are feeling. Write down the things you are saying to yourself. For example, *I'm a horrible friend* or *I am a screw-up*.

Next, try to figure out whether you're feeling shame or guilt. Use the following questions to help you figure it out:

Am I feeling bad about what I did or said in a specific situation? If yes, then it's probably guilt.

Am I feeling like I'm a bad person in a general? If yes, then it's probably shame.

Am I feeling helpless to change? If yes, then it's probably shame.

At this point, you don't need to try to change the shame, just recognize that you are feeling it. It also helps to notice where in your body you're feeling the emotion. Many people experience shame in their gut (stomach), chest, and cheeks. Just notice if you are feeling flushed, if you have trouble making eye contact with others, or if your chest or stomach feels tight. Everyone carries shame differently, and the first step is to identify the thoughts and body sensations associated with it.

Changing Shame into Guilt

All of us experience moments of shame. And as we've learned, that's not a bad thing. Shame makes us think about how we might be impacting others. The key is not staying stuck in shame, or you will keep making the same mistakes again and again. Over time, that will take a toll on your relationships, and you won't feel good about yourself. You also won't be able to feel like you can take on stressful situations, make mistakes, and learn from them—which is important for resilience.

There are several steps involved in learning to change shame into guilt. One place to start is getting better at identifying our own emotions of shame and guilt. We can't change something if we don't know it's happening. Shame is sneaky. It sometimes creeps in when we least expect it, so the first thing is to get good at learning to monitor it.

Another important step in this process involves figuring out whether setbacks are in our control. Sometimes, we just let life happen to us, and we don't spend much time trying to learn from the past. Resilient people don't experience fewer setbacks—they just use them as chances for reflection and growth.

WHAT WAS MY ROLE?

Think about the last few weeks or months of your life. Try to think about a setback you experienced. Maybe you didn't get a grade that you wanted, or you had a fight with a friend, your parents, or your girlfriend or boyfriend. As you think about what led to the outcome, try to figure out what part of the situation you could control. Use the following scale from 0 to 100.

0	50	100
I had no control over this outcome	I had some control	This was all because of my choices

If you're dealing with a situation where you have very little control, it doesn't make sense to spend time trying to figure out what else you can do. In this case, you might decide to talk to the people who have control (for example, your parents or teachers) about how they can help you deal with the setback.

If you do feel that you have at least some control, this is where you can brainstorm about what you can do in the future. You can write down the answers to the following questions in a notebook or on your phone to help you get started:

One thing I would do differently in the future is…

What I learned from this situation is…

One mistake I won't make again is to…

As you answer these questions, make sure you are referring to things that *you* can change. Remember, you cannot control anyone else's behavior or responses. Eventually, you want to learn to focus on positive, specific steps you can take for yourself.

Let's say that you heard that one of your friends was saying mean things about you. You felt hurt and so you started saying bad things about them to other people. Now everyone in your friend group is not getting along. When you look at this situation, it's less helpful to say, "One thing I learned from this situation is that I can't trust my friends" and more specific to say, "One thing I would do differently in the future is talk to my friends directly the moment I hear they are talking about me." In the second example, you are giving yourself something very specific you can do next time, which is a great way to build your resilience skills.

After you have learned to identify shame and figure out what you can learn from everyday setbacks, the next step is learning to transform shame into guilt. This is particularly useful around bigger issues—things you've done that you may not be proud of. For example, maybe you stood by idly when someone was being bullied (or maybe you participated in bullying), maybe you blamed someone for something you did, or maybe you broke someone's trust. It's not easy to look at ourselves honestly. But if you have the courage to start doing this, you can learn a lot.

And remember that you are not alone. Everyone says and does things they regret. And although we may never feel good about those things, what we do about our mistakes is also extremely important.

OWNING A FAILURE

Think back to a time when you've done something you are not proud of. This can be something that causes you shame. Maybe you hurt someone's feelings or did something that you know was really wrong. Take a few breaths and just allow yourself to feel the emotions. You can close your eyes and count to ten, just allowing yourself to feel bad, knowing you are going to learn to transform this emotion. You can do this by taking responsibility and creating a plan for the future. Here are a few ways to take responsibility. Find ways that work for you.

- **Write down what you would do differently.** Make sure you include details about what you could say differently, what you would do, or who you would talk to. Be as specific as you can.

- **Talk with a trusted friend or adult.** Tell them what you would do differently. Ask for their perspective and imagine yourself handling things differently based on their feedback.

- **Talk to someone you have hurt.** Remember, the point of shame is to help us have better relationships. Let the person know that you are sorry and that you have decided you can handle things differently in the future. Tell them what you will do differently. Be as specific as you can. This way, you are changing shame into guilt, which is a much more manageable emotion.

Now that you have explored something very difficult, you might be struggling with how to forgive yourself. Resilient people make mistakes too. They just know how to get *unstuck* from those moments. If we don't learn how to forgive ourselves, we will keep beating ourselves up for the same mistakes. And if we keep doing that, we are more likely to make the same mistakes again and again.

It's not easy to forgive ourselves for things we could have done better. Sometimes shame lives so deeply inside of us that we don't want to let it go. We might think that shame is going to help us be a better person, but often it only makes us feel worse. And when we feel worse, we can't learn or improve. The following exercise will help you explore ways to forgive yourself.

FORGIVENESS RITUALS

If you are struggling to forgive yourself for something, consider putting some of the following statements in an electronic reminder or in a notebook. Get creative and edit the statements so that they fit your needs. You can write about the situations when you are most likely to feel shame and think about what you would tell a friend if they were handling something similar. Here are some statements to get you started:

Shame doesn't help me be a better person, it keeps me stuck.

Forgiving myself isn't the same thing as letting myself off the hook.

I can learn from my mistakes, just like everyone else can.

Now, if you have incidents that are really bothering you, consider ways you can learn a lesson and then let it go. You may find that learning from your mistakes and doing things differently helps you develop better relationships with friends and family, helps you feel better about yourself, and helps you grow and change during stressful times. The focus is on learning from the situation, not letting go of the guilt entirely. These suggestions below help you identify the lessons learned from difficult incidents and let go of harsh self-judgment (shame).

- **Write and let go.** Grab a pen and two sheets of paper. Write about the incident on one sheet, and on the other write out what you want to do better. Rip up the paper describing the incident, and just hold on to what you learned.

- **Use symbolic imagery.** If you prefer art, consider taking some photos or painting, expressing how you might handle a difficult situation in the future. For example, if you want to learn to listen better, maybe you can paint or take a picture of a tree blowing in the wind, symbolizing how the tree is adjusting to nature (the wind) while still standing strong (your own personality).

- **Create a forgiveness metaphor.** Use your imagination to visualize getting some relief from the shame and picture forgiving yourself. You can imagine taking off a really heavy backpack, feeling relieved that you can breathe easier without the weight. Or imagine a beach that is littered with seaweed, shells, and human footprints; then a wave comes and washes across the sand, leaving it once again smooth. Remind yourself that you get to keep the lessons from the past *and* begin a new chapter.

A Special Note About Shame and Trauma

This skill has focused on setbacks that are at least partially in your control, things in retrospect you feel you could have handled differently. If you've experienced very difficult things in your life—perhaps you have been the victim of abuse, discrimination, a violent crime, or constant bullying—you may also be experiencing feelings of shame. Sometimes, survivors of these kinds of traumas believe they are damaged or unworthy—which is closely linked with shame. This is not the kind of shame we want to transform into guilt, because these kinds of events are not your fault.

No one ever deserves to be the victim of abuse, bullying, or a crime. These things are never your fault. If you are struggling with feelings of shame around these kinds of events, it's important for you to seek help. Skill 6 talks about professional treatment of depression and anxiety, and skill 7 talks about finding a good support system. These skills will be especially helpful if you're struggling with shame that is related to trauma. Please don't do it alone. There are many people who want to and can help.

Resiliency Recap

Everyone makes mistakes. The trick is to learn and grow from our mistakes—and not let them define us. When we experience shame about something we've done, we tend to judge ourselves really harshly. These kinds of global judgments about who we are can lead to shame. Guilt, on the other hand, has a lot more to do with the situation. When we feel guilt, we're still taking responsibility, but we're figuring out how we can handle things differently in the future. That's an important resilience skill.

You can transform shame into guilt by learning to notice shame when you're feeling it, transforming shame statements into more situation-specific guilt statements, taking responsibility for things you can change, and forgiving yourself for the past.

Although it's still not a pleasant emotion, guilt is a lot more useful if we're going to grow and change based on our past experiences. The great news is that by learning this skill as a teen, you will have a totally different way of looking at the mistakes you might make in the future.

Managing Depression and Anxiety

Feeling worried or down is a normal part of life. Everyone goes through times when they are upset. You might feel defeated or tense about your grades, your friendships, romantic relationships, or your family. Sometimes you might think about the past or worry about how uncertain the future might feel.

These feelings are signs that you're human—everyone experiences them. Yet, when we look around us, we notice that some people are able to deal with difficult feelings without getting overwhelmed. Resilient people feel emotions—lots of them—but they also understand how to cope with difficult emotions and when to seek help. This section will help you be more resilient when it comes to your feelings. You'll learn how to manage mild to moderate levels of anxiety, plus some steps to take if you think you need more help.

The first step is to understand more about these common emotions. Emotions usually consist of three different pieces:

- What we are feeling (body sensations)

- What we are thinking (thoughts)

- What happens in our bodies (feelings)

All three of these things are connected, and they influence each other. We will see how thoughts, feelings, and behaviors are all related to experiences of anxiety and depression.

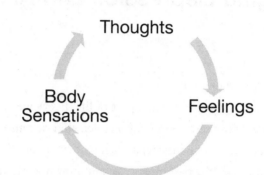

Understanding Anxiety

Anxiety is a very basic emotion. If you think about it, anxiety helps you survive. When you cross the street, you look both ways (hopefully). If you step onto the street and hear a car coming, you will step back onto the curb before you even have a chance to think about it. That is because a rush of anxiety causes your heart to race, your palms to sweat, and your pupils to dilate. Before you know it, your body is moving to get you to a safe place. So anxiety actually helps you anticipate danger.

But anxiety becomes a problem when you experience it all the time, when it overwhelms you. You might feel as if your thoughts are racing, or that you're afraid to do things that are safe, or worry about what might happen in everyday life.

It helps to understand how to describe and identify anxiety. Remember, feelings are usually one word and sum up what we are experiencing. When people are anxious, they might also describe themselves as:

- Worried
- Tense
- Nervous

- Stressed
- Fearful

When we have these kinds of feelings, our thoughts also reflect that anxious state. Some anxiety thoughts include:

I know something bad is going to happen.

I'm afraid to do this.

I can't handle what might happen.

I'm not going to be able to breathe.

I'm going to make a fool of myself.

At the same time, our bodies are reacting to this anxiety in various ways, including:

- Racing heart
- Sweating
- Shaking

- Dizziness
- Stomachache
- Shortness of breath

Your thoughts, feelings, and body sensations tend to feed off of each other, meaning that they're a cycle. For example, if you feel calm, you are more likely to tell yourself, *I feel good,* which means your face muscles might be more relaxed. If you tighten up your stomach and start to breathe really fast, you might notice yourself feeling more anxious, and you might tell yourself, *I'm not feeling good.* If you change just one thing—your thoughts, behaviors, or body sensations—it's likely that the other parts of the cycle will change too.

Understanding Sadness and Depression

Everyone experiences *sadness*. You might feel sad after a day-to-day disappointment—for example, you find out your crush doesn't like you back. Or you might feel sad over something bigger—for instance, when a good friend moves away. Human beings experience sadness because we are social animals. We have bonds that connect us to each other—to friends and family. And human beings are also able to feel happiness and joy when we accomplish something.

When something doesn't turn out the way we hoped or expected, sadness is one of many emotions we might feel. Some research suggests that sadness makes us more motivated to change situations we don't like and to pay attention to details (Forgas 2014). So sadness is something that is perfectly natural and even helpful.

Depression, on the other hand, is a prolonged period of feeling down or hopeless. When you are depressed, you might find that your eating and sleeping habits are disrupted, and you might have trouble enjoying your life.

Remember that emotions consist of feelings, thoughts, and body sensations that all influence each other. In terms of feelings, when people are experiencing sadness, they might describe themselves as:

- Down
- Blue
- Unhappy
- Miserable
- Brokenhearted
- Gloomy
- Hopeless

When you're sad, you may have thoughts like:

I feel so awful.

Things will never get better.

I'm all alone.

My heart hurts.

I can't face this.

I'm so exhausted.

In terms of your body, you may be experiencing:

- Crying
- Fatigue
- Headache
- Stomachache

If you are dealing with feelings of depression or anxiety, remember that you are not alone.

Here are some key facts about depression:

- About 12 percent of adolescents have experienced *major depression*, which involves several weeks or more when they felt depressed.

- Nearly 32 percent of adolescents have experienced an anxiety disorder, including panic attacks and being afraid of specific things (specific phobia) or social situations (Merikangas et al. 2010).

Many adolescents struggle with these issues, but many also go on to have lives that are filled with great things—including good relationships, a sense of achievement in school, and enjoyable hobbies. The key is learning how to use these mental health challenges as an opportunity for growth.

Mental Health as Self-Care

It's easy to assume that maintaining your mental health isn't something you should have to put effort into. However, that's not true. Consider this: we know that in order to stay physically healthy, we must eat a balanced diet and get some exercise. If we don't, we run the risk of all sorts of problems as we get older—including obesity, heart problems, arthritis, and diabetes.

The same is true with our emotional health. Resilient people pay attention to this aspect of their lives too, because untreated depression and anxiety make it even more difficult to cope when life gets stressful (Min et al. 2013). People who regularly take care of themselves—eating well, sleeping enough, reaching out to friends, journaling to reflect on their thoughts and actions—are more resilient during tough times. They also aren't afraid to seek help if they need it.

In general, a certain amount of sadness and anxiety is perfectly normal. Everyone experiences unhappiness and worry from time to time. These feelings only become a problem when they become extremely intense and last for several weeks or longer. If you are experiencing some sadness and anxiety, and also have feelings like happiness, joy, excitement, love, and enthusiasm, you are probably doing okay. It's important for everyone to learn how to cope with occasional feelings of sadness or nervousness.

However, if strong, negative feelings are dominating your days, you may want to consider more resources, like therapy or other community support. The exercises below will help guide you through coping skills for mild to moderate levels of sadness and anxiety, and will help you decide whether you need more guidance.

WHAT AM I FEELING?

You might be wondering whether the amount of anxiety or sadness you experience is "normal." Although there is no absolute rule, one way is to check in on your feelings a few times a day. The easiest way to do this is to set a reminder on your phone two or three times a day. Choose a time when you will have a minute or two to send yourself a quick text or jot down a few notes. When you get your reminder on your phone to check on how you're feeling, write down:

1. What you are feeling

2. A few thoughts you are having

3. How your body is feeling

If you are feeling something very intensely, make sure you put that in your notes too. You can indicate a really intense emotion with a plus sign: +. So, for example, "+Sad" means "intensely sad" and "+Disappointed" means "really disappointed." Do this for four or five days in a row.

After several days, look at what you've written down. Are at least half the feelings positive, including things like happiness, excitement, and calm? Do you have lots of intense emotions? If you are feeling that most of your emotions are negative and very intense, take a look at Do I Need More Help? at the end of this section.

Once you identify what you're feeling, you can decide how you want to handle it. If you are feeling mild to moderate levels of sadness or anxiety often, you might want to experiment with some techniques to feel better.

One way you can change what you're feeling is to change your thoughts. This technique works well when you're dealing with mild levels of anxiety or sadness that aren't affecting your ability to function. If you're still able to go to school, concentrate, make friends, and have fun, but you still occasionally feel worried or down, this technique might work well for you.

For example, Anne sometimes gets worried that she doesn't have a lot of friends. Sometimes, she finds herself thinking, *Everyone is more popular than me. It seems like I never get invited to places.* When this happens, she reminds herself that this thought isn't 100 percent true. She then corrects herself and thinks, *I do have a few close friends who always include me in things. And I'm sure everyone feels left out sometimes.* When she thinks about the situation differently, she feels less anxious and more able to enjoy the friendships she already has. She's also less self-conscious when she talks to acquaintances, because she is less worried about how they are going to judge her.

THOUGHTS AND REWARDS

One way you can learn to cope with mild levels of anxiety and sadness is to figure how you can change your thinking and behaviors. The next time you feel sad or worried, try using the following techniques to change your thoughts slightly and see whether they help the feeling pass more quickly.

- **Remind yourself that feelings change.** Try adding the phrase "for now" or "right now" to the end of your thought. For example, "I am so worried" becomes "I am so worried, for now." This helps you realize that your emotion won't last forever.

- **Try getting some distance from your feeling.** Take a deep breath while you're experiencing your difficult emotion. Then add the phrase "and I am breathing" to the end of your thought. For example, "This is so disappointing, and I am breathing." The use of the word "and" will help you realize that you can experience more than one feeling or sensation at a time. The breath may also help you change your body's response to the feeling.

- **Remember your strengths.** When you're experiencing a difficult emotion like anxiety or sadness, remind yourself of a similar situation that you dealt with successfully. Some examples: "The last time I was sad, I called my sister and it helped." "The last time I was this worried, I did fall asleep eventually." This helps you realize that you do have the skills needed to get through the situation.

- **Challenge negative assumptions.** If your thought involves expecting the worst in a situation, think about a time when the worst didn't happen. For example, "The last time I felt like everyone was talking about me, a few people did care and reached out to me to see if I was okay." This helps you challenge your assumption that the worst outcome is bound to happen.

Another useful technique is to use a reward to help you overcome mild levels of sadness or anxiety. For example, if you don't feel like facing a situation, promise yourself that if you deal with it head-on, you will give yourself a small reward. Here are some examples:

- If you are worried about asking your teacher for extra help, promise yourself some extra time to hang out with your friends if you face your fear.

- If you are feeling down about your time at your last track practice, treat yourself to a relaxing bath afterward—even if your running time doesn't improve.

Another way to boost your mood and get motivated is to reward yourself for the effort—regardless of the outcome. You deserve rewards just for trying!

Taking a closer look at your thoughts and using rewards to motivate yourself are good ways to deal with mild levels of sadness or anxiety. Another option is to learn to get some distance from your feelings, until they pass naturally. There is balance between trying to change your feelings and just allowing them to pass. Let's look at how this works for Jen.

Holding Herself to a High Standard: Jen's Story

Jen is a sixteen-year-old sophomore who's been on the track team since middle school. She's hoping to get a scholarship to a great college and become a lawyer like her mom. She's a good student and is active in a lot of clubs. But Jen puts a lot of pressure on herself. For example, she entered an essay contest, and she was really disappointed when she didn't win. She ran for student council and received enough votes to become the secretary; she was hoping to become president.

Most of the time, Jen takes these things in stride. She's able to tell herself, "When you try lots of things, you can't win them all." Reframing her thoughts in this way works for her most of the time. But sometimes, she finds herself getting worried or down about her future. At some point, Jen realizes that because she holds herself to a such a high standard, she's probably going to have days when she feels worried or upset.

What helps her get through these times is letting herself feel the ways that she feels, without judgment. Jen loves to swim, so she imagines herself on a lifeguard chair, watching her thoughts of stress or disappointment crashing on the shore like waves. Then she watches them receding.

Just like Jen used this skill to deal with her worries, you can use this kind of visualization when you feel like you can't change your thoughts. It helps you get some distance from them, making them less painful. The next exercise explores this approach.

LET IT SCROLL, ROLL, OR BLEND IN

The next time you are sad or anxious, try a few of the following techniques, which allow time and space for your feelings without having you get totally caught up in their content.

- **Let your thoughts scroll.** Close your eyes and picture your thoughts and feelings like social media posts. Imagine yourself scrolling and reading them. Now picture yourself scrolling to the next post about some other thought. If you go back to the original post, that's fine. Just allow yourself to read it until it passes, until you are no longer interested in the content and your thoughts naturally move on.

- **Let your thoughts roll.** Imagine that you are driving a bus. From your seat up front you can see all of your thoughts and feelings pass by on billboards. When the bus slows down or stops, you will experience the emotion more strongly. You also know that the bus will pick up speed again, and you will experience something else.

- **Let your thoughts blend in.** Think of your difficult emotions like dandelions. As you are experiencing them, they feel like they are unwanted weeds. But as you move back and look at your yard from a distance, you see that the dandelions mix in with many other plants and flowers. You can see grass, some weeds, some beautiful flowers, and some strong trees. They all represent different feelings that blend together in a beautiful garden. You can walk up and take a close look at the dandelion—noticing how it looks, feels, and smells. Whenever you want, you can also back up and see how it fits into the larger picture of the garden.

Mild levels of anxiety and sadness happen to everyone. If you are experiencing higher levels of negative emotions, it's important to get support before it builds up over time. Resilience doesn't mean that you never need help. Instead, it means you know when you need to reach out for help. Skill 7 talks more about social support, but when it comes to possible depression or an anxiety disorder, it's best to get support from a parent, teacher, or therapist. The Resources at the end of this book list hotlines and websites where you can find more information.

DO I NEED MORE HELP?

It can be hard to know whether you need more help to manage depression or anxiety. Think about how you have been feeling in the past month. If you answer yes to any of the questions below, you should consider reaching out to someone: a parent or trusted adult, a teacher, or a therapist.

- ☐ I have had trouble falling asleep or staying asleep several times a week.

- ☐ I struggle with overeating or a lack of appetite.

- ☐ I have felt hopeless much of the time.

- ☐ Anxiety keeps me from doing certain things (for example, meeting new people, meeting deadlines, concentrating).

- ☐ I feel extremely tired or drained, even though I haven't been sick.

- ☐ I have had thoughts of hurting myself or someone else.

→ If you answered yes to the last question, please seek help immediately. Do not struggle alone. If you do not know who to talk to, the Resources section at the back of this book lists several hotlines you can call.

These are important questions to ask yourself throughout your life. One thing resilient people do is treat their mental health with as much care as their physical health. Take time to check in with yourself every few weeks and see how you are feeling. And don't be afraid to reach out for help if you need it.

If you are struggling with how to talk about these issues with a trusted adult, consider saying some of the following conversation starters:

Do you have some time to give me some advice?

I've noticed that I've had some trouble _____ [eating, sleeping, paying attention, or whatever you are struggling with] recently, and I could really use some help.

I worry my stress might be interfering with my _____ [concentration, work, friendships, sleeping, or whatever you are struggling with]. I don't think I can handle this alone and could use some suggestions.

I've been feeling really _____ [worried, anxious, down, hopeless, or whatever your feelings are] lately, and I want your help.

If you are struggling with depression or anxiety, try to talk to someone and see what resources are available for you. Resilient people don't take on the tough times all alone, and you don't need to either.

Resiliency Recap

While we might wish that we never experienced negative emotions, that's not realistic. Life is full of situations that make us nervous or sad. In fact, anxiety helps keep us from taking crazy chances (like crossing the street without looking), and sadness helps bond us to people we love (so we miss people when they aren't with us).

The key to resilience is taking your mental health seriously. It's about learning ways to cope with the small stuff *and* also learning that it's brave to seek help when you need it.

PART III

Engaging with the World Around You Every Day

Engaging with the world around you every day	Caring for your physical health
Resilience	
Finding meaning, joy, and purpose	Caring for your mental and emotional health

Creating Safe Connections

When life gets difficult, it's hard to survive alone. We all need people to talk to when we are down and share our frustration or worries. We also need people around us to celebrate our successes and laugh with us. The ability to form and nurture safe, trusting connections is a key resilience skill. Forming stable and nurturing connections is also called finding *social support.*

---

so·cial (Merriam-Webster 2020h)

1: Involving allies or confederates.

2: Marked by pleasant companionship with friends or associates.

---

sup·port (Merriam-Webster 2020i)

1: To uphold or defend as valid or right.

2: Assist, help.

When you look at the words "social" and "support," you see that—together—they describe the people who support you when you need it. Social support can help protect or buffer you during difficult times. Many studies suggest that social support helps you when you are anxious or depressed, improving your mental health. There is even evidence that people with good social support have fewer cardiovascular problems later in life (Leigh-Hunt et al. 2017). A strong social support network not only changes your outlook but it can also positively impact your physiology.

Here are two key facts about social support:

- Compared to previous decades, adolescents are less likely to spend time socializing with each other in person and more likely to report feeling lonely (Twenge, Spitzberg, and Campbell 2019).

- Loneliness can affect the quality of your sleep and your immune system, and can leave you at risk for depression (Cacioppo, Hawkley, and Thisted 2010; Pressman et al. 2005).

Being a teenager is hard. One of the things you might be struggling with is when you should ask people for help, and when you need to learn to do things on your own. For example, should you talk to people about feeling nervous about an upcoming test? Should you lean on your parents to help you with your college applications? Should you bother other people when you can't seem to get over a bad breakup?

Our culture has an emphasis on being independent, but we know that resilient people have a strong social support network to fall back on. Resilient people know how to do things on their own, but they also know when to ask for help.

This section will help you explore how to develop those skills. If you build strong relationships when times are good, you will have a supportive network to help you out when times are stressful. The first step is to understand more about the types of social support—because not everyone gives you the same kind of support.

What Are the Kinds of Social Support?

There are many kinds of social support (Uchino 2004).

Emotional support describes the kind of support you need when you are feeling worried, sad, irritated, or angry. This is the kind of support that requires people who listen well and can be sympathetic during times of stress.

Instrumental support describes the kind of support you need when something has to be done. For example, maybe you broke your leg and need a ride to school, or you were sick and need a friend to share their math notes with you.

Informational support is the kind of support you need when you want to know more about something. When you need to make a decision, you might seek out people who can provide you with useful, accessible information and resources; these resources could include books, websites, community services, and even someone's personal experiences.

Companionship support consists of friends who give you a sense of fun and belonging.

Not every occasion calls for the same kind of social support. You may want to be around people and have fun, while at other times you may want to be around people who will listen to your problems. The key is finding a good balance of people.

Too Much Fun: Anita's Story

Anita is a freshman in high school and is active in cheerleading and dance. She is well liked and included in many parties. Her friends are fun to be around, and they often go shopping together, attend football games, or walk to the local movie theater. The girls love to talk about boys they are crushing on and the teachers they dislike. Anita feels a sense of belonging with this group.

However, when her parents decide they are getting a divorce, Anita starts to experience a deep sense of sadness and anxiety about the future. She wants to talk about it with her friends, but she realizes that since they mostly go out in large groups, there is rarely any time to talk about more serious things. She worries she will ruin the mood of their hangouts and parties by talking about her feelings. Anita realizes that her social support network is mostly companionship oriented. She decides she needs to find a way to expand or change her social support.

Before you can develop a strong social support network, you need to figure out who is already in your life and what other kinds of support you might need. Anita took the time to do this, and the following exercise will show you how to map out the support in your life.

TAKE A SOCIAL SUPPORT INVENTORY

When you do this exercise, don't worry too much about the number of people in each circle. Remember, sometimes all it takes is a few people you can really count on. Think about how many people you have in your life who give you each type of support. You can simply make a list or redraw these same circles on a sheet of paper. You'll notice that sometimes people in your life give you multiple kinds of support. Here is an example.

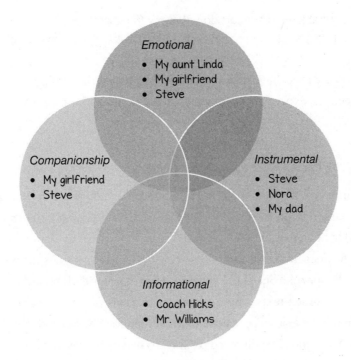

As you complete the exercise, ask yourself the following questions:

- **Do I feel like I have enough people in each of these circles?** For example, if you need a favor, do you have enough people in your *instrumental support* circle? If you want to talk about something that is bothering you, do you have enough people in your *emotional support* circle? If you have been let down in the past or been disappointed by your level of support in a circle, this section will have some suggestions for you to expand those circles.

- **Are there people who I've listed in many circles?** If so, that's great. And it's also important to take good care of these relationships. This section will also have some suggestions for how to nurture supportive relationships.

- **What kind of support do I offer my friends?** Do you want to expand what you do for people you care about, so that support is mutual?

Now that you have taken a good look at which social support circles you need to expand, you might want to consider how to grow your support.

Anita Expands Her Social Support Network

Earlier, we were discussing Anita. She felt a good sense of belonging in her larger group of friends, but when she needed emotional support around her parents' divorce, she wasn't sure who to turn to. Anita decided to try to deepen the relationships with her existing friends, as well as meet other people. She started to text a few of her friends separately and not rely on group texts. She also wondered if part of her companionship circle might be able to provide emotional support. She knew that at least two of her friends had divorced parents, so maybe they would relate. She also noticed that one of her friends was less talkative in groups but was always encouraging and positive toward other people. Anita decided to text her to see whether they could hang out sometime.

Anita also decided that she might join her school's wellness club, which focuses on mental health and stress management. Although it was out of her comfort zone, Anita took a few deep breaths and promised herself that she would attend the club at least a few times. She texted herself some encouragement, writing, "You are brave, you can do this," and looked at the text when she walked in the door of the first meeting.

Like Anita, once you have identified places to expand your social support circles, you can develop a plan for what to do next. Before we get into how to expand your network, you might be thinking about how scary or frustrating it might be to try new things. Some common worries:

What if I tell someone how I'm feeling and they don't care?

What if I ask someone for help and they don't do anything?

What if I try something new and I don't fit in?

Before you try to expand your support circles, it's important for you to give yourself some inspiration. It's hard to try new things. The next exercise will help you prepare some encouraging statements to approach new people, deepen existing relationships, and try new activities.

INSPIRING YOURSELF

This exercise has three steps. You'll need your phone (or some sort of timer) and something to write on (you can use a tablet or your phone, or paper and a pen).

1. Set the timer on your phone for five minutes. Then write down all the thoughts that hold you back when you think about: meeting new people, opening up emotionally to the people you already know, asking others for information or help, or trying out new activities. Remember that thoughts are usually full sentences. For example:

    *   People will laugh at me.

    *   I'm not good enough to join that club.

    *   My friends will think I'm dramatic.

    Continue writing down thoughts until the alarm sounds.

2. Now, set your timer for another five minutes. For each thought you wrote down, ask yourself whether it is the *worst-case* scenario or the *most likely* scenario. Challenge yourself by writing down the *most likely outcome* and the *best outcome* for each situation. For example:

    *   People will laugh at me.

- Worst outcome: Yes

- Most likely outcome: People will listen and try their best to help. Some of it might be helpful.

- Best outcome: I might feel a lot better talking about this.

3. Now that you've identified the most likely and best outcomes in these situations, text yourself these statements or write them down. They can give you motivation when you work on expanding your social circles.

Now that you've thought about which circles to expand and have some statements ready to get your courage up, it's time to get out of your comfort zone. Congratulate yourself for being brave. Creating a good social support system is one of the best things you can do for yourself. It is something that will help you both on a regular basis and when times get hard. It means you don't have to suffer alone.

Finding a support system is better for your mental health and your physical health, because in times of stress we all need other people. The next exercise will help you find a plan that is tailored to you—to expand your social support circles in your own unique way. Remember, this is not one size fits all. Feel free to experiment with these ideas and add your own ideas too.

EXPANDING YOUR SOCIAL SUPPORT CIRCLES

Start by identifying which support circles you want to expand (emotional, instrumental, informational, or companionship) and experiment with these techniques. Choose at least one activity that is a good fit for you and send yourself a reminder text to try it out.

Emotional Support

- **Learn to spot emotionally supportive people.** Who is a good listener? Is there someone who is always cheerleading others? Try to talk to that person or send them a text once or twice a week. Don't start with heavy topics. Start with more casual conversation, and over the next few weeks and months see whether the relationship becomes deeper.

- **Join a club or an activity that is focused on emotional support.** This activity can be online, through school, or in your community. For examples, groups may focus on mental health, LGBTQ support, environmental protection, peer counseling, or community service. These kinds of activities might give you opportunities to meet interesting and caring people, and expand your network. If you think these are out of your comfort zone, try to write down a few encouraging statements, like "Everyone was the new person in the group at some point."

- **Ask for support from adults.** If you need more emotional support and the issue is serious—for example, bullying, feeling depressed or very anxious, or being harmed in some way—you might reach out to adults who are good listeners. Your school counselor, trusted teacher, coach, or a parent may be very supportive. While it's nice to have peers to support you, it's also important to have trusted adults in your emotional support circle for when things get really tough. The Resources section of this book also has suggestions for professional support.

Instrumental Support

- **Learn to spot helpers.** Look out for people who volunteer to help others. These might be the folks who volunteer at a school open house or at the library. They might be the ones who organize the charity candy sales or a school dance. If you need a favor, ask them to help you out. And make sure you volunteer to help them in return.

- **Volunteer to help others.** One way to get more instrumental support is to be of service to others. Once a day, try to do something nice for someone. Text a sick friend and volunteer to send them notes from the class they missed. Ask a friend if they need a ride to the game. If you are the one who offers, it's more likely others will help you out when it's needed.

Informational Support

- **Decide what information you need.** Perhaps you need support around applying to college. Or maybe you need help trying to get yourself organized. When you can be specific about what information you need, you can more easily figure out who to approach for help.

- **Seek out mentors.** Perhaps you have counselors, parents, teachers, or coaches who can offer you information and resources. You can also reach out to other people your age who are going though similar situations. In addition, you can seek out people online, for example, groups on social media who are interested in similar topics. Send a potential mentor an email or text saying, "I noticed you know a lot about this topic. I was hoping we could talk more."

Companionship Support

- **Pay attention to who you have fun with.** Try to spot the people you like being around and the people who make you laugh. Although all relationships go through ups and downs, these are people who are generally easy to be around. Try to text one or two people and plan activities with them that are low stress—like going to the movies or grabbing coffee. If you feel less pressured in groups, consider responding more to group chats and hanging out with bigger groups of friends.

- **Increase the activities you enjoy.** These can be sports, games, or hobbies. Find noncompetitive activities in your community or at school, and make a commitment to yourself to go to at least three meetings or events. That is enough time to get past your initial worries and start to see whether you are really having fun.

During the next few weeks and months, see whether you can start to expand your social support circles. Try to check in with yourself every week and decide whether you want to try something different or keep some of your newfound activities going.

The Importance of Good Relationships

As you are going through these exercises, you might notice that certain people play an important role in your support circles. Perhaps they provide a lot of one type of support. For example, maybe you can always count on your neighbor to help offer you a ride when the bus is late. Or maybe your best friend is always there to listen when you are down. In addition, you might have someone who provides multiple forms of support in your life. For example, maybe your uncle is a great source of information about applying for college scholarships, he is always making you laugh, and he never misses your baseball practice.

Sometimes we forget to take special care of these kinds of relationships. Resilient people invest in and appreciate these kinds of relationships. In times of trouble, these are the people you might need the most. It's important to acknowledge them.

APPRECIATE YOUR ALL-STARS

Start by identifying the people you can always count on. Maybe they provide a lot of support in one area, or they provide support in multiple areas. Take a look at the list below and feel free to add it to. Do something once a month to acknowledge the supportive people in your life.

- ☐ Send your friends an email, text, or card just telling them that they are important to you.

- ☐ Send your friend a small gift or leave it at their doorstep. Include a note telling them why that gift seemed so perfect for them.

- ☐ Write your friend a note listing three things you think are great about them.

- ☐ Volunteer to do something nice for them, like helping them shovel their snow or clean their room.

It's important to make people feel loved and appreciated. It might also lift your own mood to do something nice for people you care about. On the other side of this, you might also find that there are people in your life who are not supportive. It's equally important to figure out how to manage those relationships.

Dealing with Unsupportive, Hurtful, or Abusive Relationships

Relationships are not perfect. It's normal for people to fight, hurt each other's feelings, or have times when they get annoyed or irritated with each other. But when you start to really look at your relationships, you might find people who are not contributing to your physical or emotional well-being.

Some relationships are *unsupportive*; when you turn to these people in times of trouble, you can't count on them. Or perhaps they don't make time to hang out with you—you feel like you are the only one making plans or suggesting things to do.

Some relationships are *hurtful*; these include people who don't make you feel good about yourself, not just once in a while but on a regular basis. These are people who don't have your best interests at heart. Perhaps they put you down or spread rumors about you. You might experience shame and self-doubt when you are around them.

Finally, some relationships are *abusive*; this includes people who harm you physically, sexually, or verbally threaten or bully you on a repeated basis. You deserve to be treated with respect. It's not always easy to figure out how to handle these kinds of relationships, but the final part of this section will give you some suggestions and guidance.

Unhealthy Control: Marissa's Case

Marissa is a seventeen-year-old junior in high school. She has been dating her boyfriend, Will, for more than a year. When they first met, Marissa was really flattered by Will's attention. He was a star football player, and his friends immediately accepted her. Marissa enjoyed the fact that she no longer had to stress about what she was going to do over the weekend—there was always a party or a date with Will.

As time progressed, Will began to become more possessive and jealous. He insists on reading the texts on Marissa's phone. He tells her that if she loves him, she will give him all her passwords. Will's friends begin to spread sexual rumors about Marissa; she often sees them make nasty comments about her online.

At first, Marissa tries to handle this by being extra nice to Will and his friends, but it becomes clear that it is not helping the situation. She is starting to realize that Will is not making her feel loved; the relationship is making her feel as if she's not worth anything. Marissa decides that she needs to get out of this situation, but she isn't sure how.

Does Marissa's relationship seem familiar? Maybe it resembles a relationship you or a friend has been in. You might be surprised to learn that Marissa is in an abusive relationship with Will. Although he doesn't hit her physically, he is emotionally abusive toward her. This kind of abuse can be just as hurtful and damaging as physical abuse. In addition, his friends are contributing to a cruel environment that involves online bullying and harassment. Marissa is smart to try to change her situation.

Not only do abusive relationships take a toll on you in the short term, but in the long term they also increase your risk for depression, anxiety disorders, and even physical health problems. If you have identified relationships that are unsupportive, hurtful, or abusive, you may need to try different strategies to distance yourself from these relationships. The following exercise has some suggestions.

LETTING GO OF UNHEALTHY RELATIONSHIPS

Close your eyes, breathe, and visualize the people in your life. Ask yourself the following questions:

Is there anyone in my life who is inconsistent? Is there someone who doesn't really show up for me in good times or bad times?

These relationships might be unsupportive.

If you are experiencing unsupportive relationships, try to distance yourself from them over time.

- Try not to respond to their calls or texts right away.

- Keep your responses to the person brief.

- Turn down invitations to socialize one on one.

- If you encounter these people in group settings, keep your conversations general and friendly, not personal.

Is there anyone in my life who constantly makes me feel bad about myself? Do they put me down, gossip about me, or make me feel unsure of myself?

These relationships might be hurtful.
If you are experiencing hurtful relationships, try to prioritize your self-respect.

- Try to minimize your voluntary interactions with the person.

- If you must interact (for example, if they are in a position of authority over you), write down some encouraging messages for yourself. For example, *I do not deserve to feel bad about myself. I do not deserve to be gossiped about.*

- If you can, let the person know how their behavior makes you feel. Enlist the help of a friend or trusted adult so you don't have to go into the situation alone. For example, you can say, "I don't want to be around people who gossip about me and others." If people respond by trying to change their behavior, you might want to give them a chance. However, if they keep slipping back to the same behavior (for example, gossiping or putting you down), you might consider distancing from the relationship (see the strategies above).

Is there anyone in my life who has abused me physically, emotionally, or sexually? Has anyone caused bodily harm to me, made threats of harm, or constantly makes me feel afraid or demeaned?

These relationships are abusive.
If you are experiencing abusive relationships:

- Please do not suffer alone. There is help for you.

- Reach out to a trusted adult and ask for help. This may be a teacher, coach, or counselor. Perhaps you can talk to a friend's parent, a neighbor, or someone at your community center or church.

- The Resources section of this book also lists places you can call for help. You are not alone.

Once you start thinking through your relationships and identifying anyone who is unsupportive, harmful, or abusive, you can figure out an individualized plan of how to handle things. For example, Marissa wanted to break up with her boyfriend. But she was worried that if she left him, the situation would escalate and his friends would increase their online bullying.

In situations that involve physical or emotional abuse, it is extremely important to find a trusted adult to help you deal with the situation safely. Marissa wisely decided that she could not handle the situation alone. She contacted her school counselor, who was trained in helping teens overcome dating violence. The counselor was able to involve both Marissa's and Will's parents to form a plan to end the relationship without anyone being harmed. Marissa also started counseling with a local therapist to talk about her sadness and confusion about the relationship ending. In the long term, these supports will help Marissa build her resilience. If she talks about her feelings now, she is much more likely to find healthy friendships and relationships in the future.

Social Support Is Always Changing and Takes Planning

Finding people who support you—when you need to talk, need a favor, need information, and need to have fun—is a continual process. Relationships are always changing. Sometimes you are close to someone emotionally, but then life changes and you drift apart. Maybe your close friend gets very busy and can't provide you with the same support that they used to. Maybe a neighbor who always helped you out moved away. Perhaps a coach who was a great mentor gets a job at a different school.

Resilient people invest in their social support networks but also realize that those networks might change over time. It's important to check in with yourself periodically. Once a year—or more often, if you'd like—ask yourself who is in your social support circles and see whether you need to do things to improve your relationships.

In addition, plan ahead for when you might need more support. Think specifically about the type of support you need, and then try to ask for it. For example, when you look at the semester ahead of you, maybe you know the month of May is going to be jammed with volleyball practice and studying for finals. Maybe you ask your mom if she could help do your laundry on those weekends; or maybe you ask a friend if they want to watch a funny movie every Saturday in May for some stress relief.

It's important to surround yourself with people who are good to you—and who you can be good to in return. Taking good care of our relationships is one of the most important resilience skills, because other people can offer us comfort, companionship, information, and help when we need it—and we all have times when we need support.

Resiliency Recap

No one can get through tough times alone. Human beings are wired for connection. Those connections take many forms. Sometimes they involve deep conversation, and sometimes they involve a simple favor. Sometimes we need people to mentor us and give us information, and at other times we just want to hang out with friends and have fun.

It's important to nurture all of these support circles and to try new things if you need to expand those circles. Finally, it's important to appreciate people who are supportive and let go of relationships that are not healthy. Taking care of your relationships will help you enjoy your daily life more and will also help you in times of stress. Good relationships are worth their weight in gold.

Active Coping for Taking Healthy Chances

Life is not fun if we never get out of our comfort zone. It's normal and healthy to want to try new things—to meet new people, try different activities, and even take some risks. Nobody wants every day to be the same. When you don't take any chances, you risk feeling bored. You also might feel down and depressed, or worried that you are missing out on something fun. The more you avoid new situations, the more nervous you get when you think about doing something new. You start to doubt yourself all the time.

As you can see, this is a vicious cycle. While staying in your comfort zone protects you from experiencing anxiety, disappointment, or rejection, it also means you will miss out on new experiences that you might really enjoy!

A key resilience skill is *active coping*, which involves a thoughtful and balanced way of taking chances and planning.

---

ac·tive (Merriam-Webster 2020a)

1: Characterized by action rather than by contemplation or speculation.

2: Producing or involving action or movement.

---

cop·ing (Merriam-Webster 2020c)

1: Dealing with and attempting to overcome problems and difficulties.

Active coping involves finding healthy, resourceful ways to deal with problems. Active coping can help you face problems in small, manageable steps, before they become overwhelming. You can use active coping to help you when you feel anxious about a situation and to help you plan ahead for situations that might be risky.

Why Avoidance Doesn't Work

When you are faced with problems in life, it's very tempting to ignore them. Maybe you're worried about your grade in Spanish class but don't want to email your teacher to ask questions. The more you put off talking to your teacher, the worse your grade gets. The worse your grade gets, the more you're likely to be embarrassed to talk to your teacher. See how avoiding the problem becomes a downward spiral?

Maybe you want to try out for the debate team, but you worry that you won't make it. So you decide not to try out, because you don't want to deal with possible disappointment. A few weeks later, you decide you want to try a new activity—singing. But when it's time to audition for choir, you're completely stressed out—because you haven't had any experience with successfully managing your nerves. You become convinced you aren't the type of person who can do new things, causing a downward spiral.

The good news is that we don't have to get caught in these patterns. We have many options to try new things in a healthy, safe, and manageable way. This is called *systematic desensitization* and it's an important way we can learn to take thoughtful chances.

Systematic Desensitization

Think about how we learn to swim. Usually it involves lots of trips to the pool, getting familiar with the water, learning how to float, and practicing coordinating our breath with our strokes and kicks. But we've all heard of someone whose relative threw them into the deep end of the pool during their first swim lesson. Did it teach them how swim? Probably not. Usually, that just makes us even more afraid to get into the pool the next time. And that's the opposite of systematic desensitization.

What's more effective is to get used to the water slowly but steadily. Here are some key facts about trying new things and taking risks:

- Trying new things and taking risks takes planning, thinking through the consequences, and using small steps.

- Systematic desensitization is the process of facing what we are afraid of, but in manageable steps (Head and Gross 2009).

- Systematic desensitization also involves using breathing and relaxation skills to manage our anxiety when we try these steps.

Let's see how this skill fits into the life of Ben, who lost his dog in a tragic accident.

Overcoming a Traumatic Loss: Ben's Story

Ben is a fourteen-year-old who has just started high school. One day Ben is walking his dog near a busy intersection. Ben has always been careful to watch for cars, but on this particular day, a car comes speeding down the street out of nowhere. Somehow Ben loses control of the leash and, before he even has a chance to react, Ben sees his dog get hit by the car.

After his dog dies, Ben is overcome with feelings of sadness. Eventually, his family decides the time is right to adopt a new dog from the local shelter. However, Ben is initially extremely afraid to take the dog out for a walk again. He is worried he will not be able to protect the new dog, who is just a puppy.

Ben decides to use systematic desensitization to overcome his worries. He makes a list of smaller steps to build up to the long walks he used to take. The first step involves just taking the puppy into the backyard. The second step involves walking on the sidewalk without crossing the street. His third step is to cross over into a nearby park. The final step involves crossing the busy intersection.

When his anxiety level is high, Ben uses deep breathing to calm himself down. He is able to face his fear over time. After a month he is able to take his new puppy on long walks, and eventually, he even starts to relax and enjoy the walks.

Ben didn't overcome his worries right away—it was a process. You can also use the process of systematic desensitization to help you face things you've been avoiding.

FACING YOUR FEARS SLOWLY

Think about something you might be avoiding because you're afraid of what might happen. The possibilities are endless. For example, maybe you're afraid of auditioning for a play, texting someone you have a crush on, learning to parallel park the car, or applying to a college that you might not get into. Break up this big challenge into smaller parts based on how much anxiety you think you'd experience along the way. You can use as many steps as you need, depending on the situation.

Let's look at an example:

Trying out for a play—anxiety level 10

Practicing lines with someone I don't know well with strangers watching us—anxiety level 9

Practicing lines with my friend in an auditorium with strangers watching us—anxiety level 8

Rehearsing lines with my friend in an auditorium with a few of my friends watching us—anxiety level 6

Rehearsing lines with my friend—anxiety level 4

Reading a monologue in front of my mom and sister—anxiety level 3

Reading a monologue to myself—anxiety level 1

You can start by creating your own list. Write down your big challenge and break it up into smaller steps. Be sure to start at the step with the lowest anxiety and work your way up. If your lowest step still feels overwhelming, try to break it up even more. Once you've written your list, you are ready to start. Pick the lowest step that makes you least anxious and try it. Work your way up your list at your own pace (from less anxiety to more anxiety). As you attempt each step, here are a few tips:

- Make sure you breathe in and out slowly to help calm down your body. You will find that your heart rate will decrease and your muscles will feel less tense.

- Rate your anxiety when you start each step, and rate your anxiety afterward. Ideally, your anxiety level should be lower at the end of the step.

- If your anxiety level is high when you are trying a step, try to stay with it and keep breathing until your anxiety starts to come down.

- You might try the same step several times if your anxiety level is high. When a step becomes easy, that's when you know it's time to move on.

- If you feel like your anxiety level is just too high, try breaking down your steps even further.

- Don't rush yourself. As long as you keep trying to work your way up the steps, don't worry if some of the challenges on your list take you days, weeks, or even months to master.

Systematic desensitization is a useful way to help you break down huge challenges that might feel overwhelming. Remember that even the smallest of steps add up over time. So even if you are feeling as if it might take you a long time to face a challenge fully, remind yourself that every step gets you closer to your goal.

Coping with Disappointment

Another important aspect of learning to take healthy chances is accepting the fact that things don't always work out the way we want them to. Maybe you try out and don't get chosen for the team, or maybe the person you want to date isn't interested. Resilient people also experience hurt and disappointment—we all do. They just have ways to keep those feelings from overwhelming them and affecting their long-term behavior. For example, reminding yourself of your long-term goals allows you to experience difficult emotions—like rejection or disappointment—without feeling completely overwhelmed. Let's look at how disappointment affected Chris as he applied for scholarships.

Getting Used to No: Chris's Story

Chris is an eighteen-year-old senior in high school. He lives with his mom, who works two jobs to support Chris and his two younger brothers. Chris works after school at the local grocery store, and he feels good about contributing financially to the family. He gets decent grades and hopes to get enough scholarship money to pay for most of his college education.

After he applies to several foundations and colleges for scholarships, he receives many rejection letters. The letters are always respectful and encouraging, but they are still difficult and disappointing to read. But Chris manages to keep focused on his long-term goal. All he needs is one big scholarship, or a few smaller ones, to really make a difference. He keeps reminding himself that the rejections are not about him and that there may have been many factors that influenced the decisions.

Finally, Chris receives a foundation scholarship that will pay for most of his community college tuition. Chris approaches the local four-year university and talks to the admissions office—they are impressed by his scholarship and give him more money for their university. Overall, Chris's ability to persist through disappointment is key in helping him attend a university of his choice.

As we can see from Chris's story, one of the things that helped him persist in the face of disappointment was a focus on his long-term goals and values. When you are putting yourself out there and getting out of your comfort zone, it's important to remind yourself of *why* these chances are important to you. How do they influence your long-term goals? How do they relate to how you see yourself? The following exercise will help you get in touch with some of your deeper goals and values, which help motivate you when you take healthy chances.

WHAT'S IMPORTANT TO ME?

Set aside half an hour to brainstorm answers to the following questions:

1. Is there something I want to achieve or become more involved in the next year?

   Example: *I want to get all As and Bs on my report card.*

2. If I couldn't see anyone for a whole month, who would I miss the most? Which relationships are the most important to me?

   Example: *My best friend and my dad.*

3. What do I want my friends and family to say about me when I'm not with them? What are the words I'm hoping they use to describe me?

   Example: *Hardworking, persistent, funny, smart.*

Now, find a way to express these values to yourself. This is all based on your own personality and preferences. You can be as linear or as artistic as you want to be. Take a look at your answers to those questions and get inspired. Here are some suggestions, and feel free to try others:

- **Make a collage** with words that include your goals, your important relationships, and the characteristics you value.

- **Create a spreadsheet** or write down a list of goals for the next year. You can even use color coding (red for personal goals, green for academics, blue for relationships, yellow for fun, and so on).

- **Write a poem** that describes some of your goals, relationships, and characteristics.

- **Paint or draw** something that represents these ideas.

- **Create a song** or piece of dance that represents some of your goals and values.

Once you have created something that represents your long-term goals and values, keep it somewhere where you can look at it, especially when you feel nervous about taking on new challenges or trying new things. Ask yourself whether what you want to attempt fits with your overall values.

Another part of healthy risk taking is learning to cope with hurt and disappointment in a way that doesn't overwhelm you. If you're going to take healthy risks, you'll be disappointed or upset at times. That's normal. But part of resilience is learning how to get back up again and not let those emotions define you.

One useful way to cope with these emotions is to allow yourself to have them while giving yourself some encouragement at the same time. A helpful strategy is to allow yourself to experience an emotional reaction but to not let that emotional reaction dictate what you are going to do next time. The following exercise has some specific suggestions.

HOW TO HANDLE A DISAPPOINTMENT OR FAILURE

Grab some paper and a pen, or your laptop or phone. Think back to the last time something didn't work out the way you wanted it to. Write down a few sentences about the situation.

Example: I liked this guy and texted him, and he never responded.

1. Ask yourself the following questions:

   What was my emotional reaction? Example: I felt embarrassed and really upset.

What did I do next? Example: I didn't tell anyone about it. I felt too stupid.

What did I want to do next (or what would I have told a friend to do in this situation)? Example: I wanted to talk to my friends for support, but I didn't.

2. Use the word "and" to describe your *feelings* and how you might *handle* something similar in the future.

    Example: Next time I might still be upset if someone doesn't like me *and* talking to my friends might make me feel less alone. They might be able to relate to what I'm going through.

Resilience doesn't mean that you don't have emotional reactions to difficult situations or disappointments. It means that you're able to acknowledge those emotions and give yourself some good advice about what to do next. Often, thinking about what you might tell a friend is a great way to get a different perspective on a tough situation. We're often very hard on ourselves, but when it comes to people we care about, we're able to give good advice. Try to be a friend to yourself by acknowledging your own emotions and giving yourself motivation for healthy steps forward.

Once you have learned systematic desensitization, identified some values and long-term goals, and figured out ways to deal with disappointment, there is one more aspect of healthy risk taking to explore: What is healthy and what is risky? It can be hard to figure out what kinds of chances are worth taking and what might be harmful.

Planning Ahead for Risky Situations

It's important to take healthy chances—like trying out for a team, working for good grades, making new friends, or dating. But sometimes, you might wonder whether certain chances are worth taking. That is especially true for situations that might involve some kind of physical risk, such as attending a party where there might be alcohol or cannabis involved, or getting in a car with someone who isn't a very good driver.

There are two parts of our brain that influence our decision making (Linehan 1993). Our *emotional mind* is involved in how we feel about something. For example, if you think about going to a party that involves alcohol, you might be excited but also nervous about what might happen. Our *rational mind* is involved in looking at the objective facts involved in a situation. It might tell you not to go to the party because you would be breaking rules.

When your rational mind and emotional mind come together, they often form a gut feeling or intuition that guides you to do what's best. This is called *wise mind* (Linehan 1993). In this case, wise mind might tell you that you can go to the party, but you should tell your friend ahead of time that you won't get in a car with anyone who is drinking. Wise mind might help you figure out beforehand how many drinks you plan to consume. Wise mind might also suggest that you tell your parents ahead of time that you won't ever get in the car with someone who's drinking, and ask whether you can call them if you need to.

Wise mind can play an important role in bringing together the emotional aspects of your decision making with the rational pros and cons of something (Linehan 1993) to form a healthy compromise. Wise mind can help you access your best decision making and use your best supports to help you keep safe and healthy. The exercise below will help you develop your wise mind.

PLANNING AHEAD IN RISKIER SITUATIONS

Grab paper and a pen, or your laptop or phone. Think back to a situation that involved risk, either to you or someone else, such as a situation where you thought someone's physical or emotional safety might be affected. Example: *I was hanging out with a group of friends who were posting jokes online that some people think are offensive.*

1. Identify the feelings you felt at the time. Remember that feelings are usually one word or a short phrase. Write them all down. Example: Nervous, excited to be included, disappointed in myself.

2. Identify what the rational part of you was saying. These thoughts are usually in the form of sentences. Example: You might get caught. If no one gets hurt, this could be fun.

3. Take a few deep breaths and identify what your *wise mind* might have said. This is the part that brings reason and emotion together. It's the part of your mind that forms compromises. Example: This might offend someone. In the long term, this probably isn't worth it.

4. Once you have identified what your wise mind might have said in that instance, what can you learn from this situation? Example: In the future, I'll go home if they are posting things I'm not comfortable with. Depending on the content, I can tell a counselor to look at the account—if it gets really mean.

It takes a lot of practice to develop your wise mind, so don't be discouraged if this takes you some practice. You might be someone who makes a lot of your decisions based on your emotions, or you might be someone who is very rational. Learning to blend these parts of your decision making takes a while. You have to pay attention to both sides and find ways to bring them together. The more you try it, the easier it will become. With practice, you'll find that when you are unsure about a risky situation, you're able to come to a decision that integrates your safety and a good support system, while also involving fun.

Resiliency Recap

When you are faced with challenging situations, avoidance doesn't work. When life becomes challenging, learning to break down those obstacles into smaller, manageable steps (systematic desensitization) might be very useful. In addition, learning to deal with disappointment is an essential part of resilience, because everyone feels let down sometimes.

You can learn how to take healthy chances that involve your wise mind, and looking back at your challenges can help you learn from them in the future. Remember that your long-term goals and values can guide you. You have things that are important to you, people who you care about, and qualities you want to represent. When you are making decisions and taking healthy risks, always remember your goals and values—they will help guide you through life's challenges—both now and in the future.

PART IV

Finding Meaning, Joy, and Purpose

Cognitive Flexibility and Realistic Optimism

There is an old story about a gardener who is trying to grow grass on his large front lawn. Every year, the grass looks healthy, green, and strong, but after a while, the yard also starts to sprout some dandelions. At first, the gardener picks the flowery weeds out by hand. But they keep popping up. He gets some weed killer, but this kills the healthy grass, and the dandelions still find a way back into his yard. The gardener decides to pull every single dandelion, which seems to work for the remainder of the season. But the next spring, he's exasperated to see more dandelions sprout up again.

In desperation, he thinks they might be spreading from his neighbor's lawn, so he asks them to pull all their dandelions too. Nothing seems to work—the dandelions always seem to sprout up. Totally frustrated, he seeks the advice of the most experienced gardener in town. The master gardener tells him, "Sir, sometimes you just have to learn how to love those dandelions" (Nhat Hanh 2010).

This story illustrates the fact that everyone has obstacles in their lives. We can't get rid of our challenges, but we can change our perspective. Clearly, the gardener had been seeing dandelions as a weed, and he had done everything he could to make them go away. But at some point, he needed to learn how to see them as colorful flowers that were a part of his lawn.

This section will explore the concepts of *cognitive flexibility* and *realistic optimism*—two skills the master gardener used to analyze the dandelion problem—and how they relate to resilience.

Cognitive Flexibility

Cognitive flexibility is the ability to examine a situation from various points of view. Situations are often not all bad or all good, even though many of us see things that way. For example, maybe you broke a bone during soccer practice, and now you have to spend a few weeks at home. Even though it's a big setback, you find that you can use the time to get ahead on a school project that you didn't have time for. Most of the time, there are multiple ways of interpreting something. This skill can be particularly useful in times of stress.

---

cog·ni·tive (Merriam-Webster 2020b)

1: Relating to or involving conscious intellectual activity (such as thinking, reasoning, or remembering).

2: Based on or capable of being reduced to factual knowledge.

---

flex·i·bi·li·ty (Merriam-Webster 2020d)

1: The ability to yield to influence.

2: Having a ready capability to adapt to new, different, or changing requirements.

Cognitive flexibility can help you overcome obstacles during times of stress. Seeing things in a fixed way can keep you stuck, because you're unable to see other ways of solving your problems. You may get so caught up in how bad your problem is that you might start to believe there is only one way to solve it. Cognitive flexibility helps you look at a challenge from multiple viewpoints, which can help you feel like you have more choices about how to handle things.

Cognitive flexibility can also help you get some perspective *after* a challenging situation is over. It helps you understand how a tough situation has helped you grow and what you've gained. Looking at a situation from different angles can help you feel better about it, which means you are more likely to overcome future setbacks, rather than feel down or helpless. When you encounter a difficult situation, start by asking yourself challenging questions:

What has contributed to my problem?

How do I think I can solve this problem?

If I told a friend or mentor about this issue, what follow-up questions would they ask me?

Is there another way of looking at this situation?

Is there another solution that could also work? What are all my options?

Is there any positive aspect or benefit in this difficult situation, however small?

Given the situation, is there something small I can be grateful for?

Cognitive flexibility can help you transform difficult situations by thinking about them differently. For example:

Initial Thought	Flexible Thought
I can't believe I failed the test.	This gives me opportunities to figure out how I can study more effectively in the future.
I know that my friend was annoyed with me.	She might've been having a bad day in general, so I should just ask her.
It's not fair that I broke my leg and can't play this season.	It's not fair, but now that I have more time, I can start photography—something I've always wanted to try.
It was incredibly stressful to deal with this situation.	I was able to see how much strength I had.
That was a terrible situation.	I am grateful that my friend stepped in to try to help.

Cognitive flexibility can be used with small setbacks and large challenges. It can help you problem-solve during a stressful situation. It can help you calm down when a situation feels overwhelming. Let's take a look at Ava, who is dealing with returning to school after a short-term illness.

Cognitive Flexibility and Short-Term Stress: Ava's Story

Ava is a seventeen-year-old junior in high school. She is focused on getting into a good college, studies really hard, and is involved in a lot of clubs. Unfortunately, Ava is diagnosed with the flu during the second semester of her junior year and misses almost two weeks of school. She is too sick to do homework and can't maintain her regular study schedule for her advanced placement exams or college entrance tests.

When Ava goes back to school, she feels extremely anxious. She thinks it might be impossible to catch up. However, Ava realizes that she cannot change the fact that she had the flu. She knows that her body was too weak to study and that extra stress would have just made her physical health worse.

Ava decides that her best option is to focus on the future and form a realistic plan. She meets with each teacher individually to help her map out the essential things she missed. Together, they form a detailed plan of study that will help her catch up during the next month, focusing on the most important assignments first.

Although Ava was still upset about getting sick, she was also proud of the fact that she used this situation to reach out to her teachers, get to know them better, and come up with a specific plan to catch up. She realized that she didn't have to do every assignment in the order it was assigned. Her cognitive flexibility helped her solve a problem and recognize the small benefits involved in her challenge. Have you had to deal with a setback or an obstacle, and then challenged yourself to see it differently?

Thinking flexibly can help you with short-term stressors as well as longer-term, more severe setbacks. Cognitive flexibility can lead to *posttraumatic growth*, which is the ability to make meaning and find positive aspects in the most difficult situations. Take a look at how cognitive flexibility can help in a more serious or traumatic situation, such as the serious illness of a family member.

Cancer in the Family: Mark's Story

Mark is a fifteen-year-old sophomore in high school who lives with his mom and younger brother. His parents are divorced, and his dad lives several hours away. Since the divorce, Mark has had to take on a lot of responsibility at home.

Mark's mom was recently diagnosed with breast cancer. Thankfully, the doctors believe she will respond well to treatment, but the days she goes through chemotherapy are hard. Mark is worried about his mom's health, and it hurts to see her suffer. He's not able to go to friends' houses as often anymore, because his mom is too weak to drive him anywhere. He spends every day taking care of his brother and mom. Mark misses his old routine, and then feels guilty about his feelings. Sometimes, he wonders why this had to happen to his family and feels angry at the unfairness of it all.

Many friends and neighbors have organized a meal train, and several of Mark's teachers have reached out to him, volunteering to give him extra help or a sympathetic ear. As the months pass, his mom begins to feel better; she has responded well to the treatment.

Mark starts to look back at this terribly stressful time. In addition to remembering all the difficulty he endured, he starts to recall the kindness of his neighbors and his teachers. He's also impressed with his own strength, saying, "I never knew I could go to school and also help my family so much."

Mark's ability to use cognitive flexibility to understand the bigger picture of a very difficult situation is impressive. He was able to identify some positive aspects of the situation (the support of others) and also appreciate strengths within himself. Learning lessons and finding positives in difficult situations using cognitive flexibility is an extremely valuable resilience skill. If Mark had only focused on the thought "My mom got cancer and it was totally unfair," he would have missed the opportunity to appreciate the ways the situation helped him grow. This does not mean that he would choose to have this situation happen—it only means that once it did happen, he was able to look at it from every angle.

A simple way to learn cognitive flexibility is to look at your everyday challenges and identify: 1) something positive, and 2) something you learned.

VIEWING CHALLENGES DIFFERENTLY

For five minutes at the end of the day, close your eyes and think about something challenging or difficult that happened that day. It's easier if you start with situations that aren't overwhelming (or traumatic), for example: taking a difficult test, feeling bored at home, or losing a game.

Visualize the situation in detail. Who was there? What were you feeling? What were the sights and sounds around you? How did the situation end? As you visualize, ask yourself these questions:

1. What did I learn about myself in how I reacted today? Did I show any strengths?

2. What was I grateful for in this situation—either someone or something? Was there anything positive, however small?

Try to do this visualization every day for a week with a focus on identifying one strength in yourself and one aspect of the situation that was positive (or made you grateful). Once you are able to do this easily with less stressful situations, you can use this technique with more challenging, ongoing stressors like illness and trauma. Although it will not take away what you've experienced, it might help ease some of your feelings of sadness, disappointment, or anxiety.

In the case of more challenging situations, this kind of exercise doesn't mean that you have to accept or enjoy trauma and illness, it only means that you are focusing on finding ways to be kind to yourself and to acknowledge any positives in your life. Resilient people use this coping skill, along with getting social support, emotional tolerance, and taking healthy risks to help them overcome more serious problems. It takes practice to put these skills together, but over time you will find what works best for you.

Realistic Optimism

Cognitive flexibility helps you *during* and *after* a challenging situation. The concept of *realistic optimism* is closely related, but it can help you *plan ahead* for difficult times. Realistic optimism involves planning for stressful situations and also trying to find something to be hopeful for. Realistic optimism doesn't mean that you avoid negative thoughts and feelings, and it doesn't mean that you need to accept every situation as it is. Realistic optimism involves focusing on the best possible outcome *and* planning for the most realistic outcome *at the same time*. Here are some examples of how to transform your thoughts into realistic optimism about the future.

Initial Thought	Realistic Optimist Thought
I'm going to fail the test. [no optimism, no plan]	If I study for three hours, I might get an A. Even if I don't get an A, I'll probably do pretty well if I put in the effort.

If I stop worrying about my choir audition, it will all be fine. [optimism, but no plan]	If I practice a few times in front of Mom, it will help my nerves and make it more likely that I'll get the solo.
I don't think I can deal with this breakup. [no optimism, no plan]	If I talk to my friends and keep busy, it will help a lot. I'm still going to be sad, but I will have good days again.

Resilient people are able to apply the concept of realistic optimism to their everyday lives. When life becomes very stressful, this way of planning for the future—coming up with realistic goals while maintaining hope—becomes second nature to them. Ideally, cognitive flexibility and realistic optimism can be combined as a way to help you thrive. Here are some key facts about combining the two skills:

- Optimism alone can't help you when things are difficult, because your mental and physical health may be adversely affected if you continually feel let down by your expectations.

- When combined with cognitive flexibility, optimism can help you deal with serious situations, including things like violence, discrimination, and chronic illness (Iacoviello and Charney 2014).

Let's see how Jason used cognitive flexibility and realistic optimism in the following story.

I Just Want a Home: Jason's Story

Jason just turned fourteen. He is the oldest of four kids and the only son in his family. Jason will be finishing eighth grade in a few months. The apartment building that Jason's family lived in recently had a serious fire. They lost most of their possessions and had to move in with Jason's grandparents, who live several blocks from their old apartment.

Suddenly, Jason's old life is gone. He misses his old room. He's worried about the future. Over time, Jason sees everyone in the family pitching in to try to help. He notices that they all have good days and bad days—days when they are sad and days when they still laugh together.

Jason thinks about the long summer ahead, realizing that it's going to be sad for them. But he also wants to figure out a way to have some fun with his family, even while they feel sad. He wonders if there's anything he can do to make his sisters feel better. Because the family has always loved to swim together, he decides to take his sisters to the neighborhood pool several times a week. The siblings have something to look forward to and a way to have some fun— even though times are difficult.

Creating Optimism: The Importance of Everyday Joy, Fun, and Humor

Jason's story illustrates that realistic optimism can be practiced in some very tough circumstances. One way to find optimism in the most difficult times is to incorporate small moments of joy, happiness, and fun in your daily routine. That way, when you are struggling with a challenge—even a very large one—you will have something to fall back on that feels familiar, comforting, and enjoyable. The following exercise has some suggestions for bringing some happiness into your daily routine.

DO WHAT YOU LOVE

Think about something you can do that brings you joy or happiness, or makes you laugh. The key is that these activities need to be healthy and easy to do regularly (daily or almost every day). This should never feel like homework. Choose things you want to do, not things you have to do. This isn't about going outside of your comfort zone; it's about finding comfort. You don't need to be struggling with setbacks to do things you enjoy; you can do them regularly. Try any of these activities or add others to the list:

- Do something *physical* like ride your bike, swim, jog, exercise, play sports, or dance to your favorite music.

- Do something *artistic* like paint, make a collage, draw, cook, sing, listen to music, or act.

- Do something *silly* like watch a comedy skit, tell jokes, or make humorous videos.

- Do something *fun* like spend time with supportive friends.

- Do something *relaxing* like take a hot bath, practice yoga, or do a crossword puzzle.

Over the course of a week, notice which activities bring you happiness. Ideally, you should have activities from more than one category on your list (for example, something relaxing, something silly, and so on). At the end of the day, get in the habit of asking yourself, *What did I do just for me today?* Ideally, every day will include at least a little time that brings joy, happiness, humor, and fun to your day.

Hopefully, finding more ways to enjoy yourself doesn't feel like work. The trick is going easy on yourself and just experimenting with what works for you. As you begin to feel more daily happiness, you will find that realistic optimism becomes easier. You will be able to form plans and also focus on some of the best possible outcomes.

The Importance of Gratitude

Another important aspect of cognitive flexibility and realistic optimism is the ability to find something that you are grateful for, even in the most challenging times. Appreciating your blessings—however small—can help your problem-solving ability and overall mood, making it more likely that you can successfully deal with setbacks. Gratitude is an important part of resilience, because if you can see the good things in your daily life, you are more likely to be able to see the good when things are hard. For example, by noticing things to be grateful for, you might be able to find people or circumstances that can help you change or overcome a difficult situation.

Gratitude is not a fixed trait. It is a skill that can be developed with practice. The following exercise can help you focus on finding a gratitude practice that works for you.

EVERYDAY GRATITUDE

Try to do one thing each day that helps you focus on the positive aspects of life. These can be small. In fact, noticing the small things may be the most powerful form of this practice. See what works for you:

- **Write a note.** If someone has done something nice for you, send them a quick note or text to say thank you. Or send them a cute card.

- **Pay attention.** Notice the world around you—a beautiful sunset, a pretty tree, a funny-looking dog. Take a picture to remind yourself of how you enjoyed that moment.

- **Start a gratitude jar.** At home, ask every family member to write down something that they are grateful for and place their note in a gratitude jar. Every few months, read them together.

- **Make a collage.** Represent all the things that make you happy and hang it in a place where you will see it every day.

- **Appreciate your meals.** Before you eat, pause to appreciate all the people whose efforts went into getting the food on your plate—the farmer who grew the crops, the truck driver who drove it to the store, the grocery store workers who stocked the shelves, the person who prepared the food.

- **Text a friend.** Just tell them one quality you appreciate about them.

The key to any gratitude practice is that it needs to become a daily part of your life. Once you do it regularly, gratitude will become a part of the way you think. You might find that your friends and family start expressing more gratitude. You might start a tradition.

Stress and Growth

Sometimes difficult and even painful experiences can help us grow. Maybe you survived a bad breakup. And even though you wouldn't want to do it again, it makes you realize that, in the long run, you are a worthy person. Maybe you didn't get into the club you wanted. But that disappointment helped you realize that if you don't try new things, you're always going to regret not trying.

Often our biggest moments of personal growth happen because of disappointments and setbacks, not from an easy success or achievement.

Using cognitive flexibility, we learn more about our strengths and values as we work through challenges. The final exercise in this section will help you remember that setbacks are a part of growth.

HONORING YOUR STRUGGLES

Think back to a time when you struggled with something significant. Maybe a good friend moved away, you (or someone close to you) dealt with a serious illness, you had to move, or someone hurt you emotionally or physically. Try to picture yourself growing and learning from these experiences—maybe with the help of others, through your own strengths, or a combination of these factors. When you picture that growth, what do you see? Choose any method to express yourself:

- Draw a picture or paint how you envision this struggle helping you grow.

- Write about how you think this struggle can both positively and negatively influence your future.

- Talk to someone about how you think this setback has influenced you.

- Make a spreadsheet with specific goals based on this challenge.

- Write a poem that expresses how this situation has influenced you.

This is a personal process. The important thing is to appreciate the fact that your struggles have helped you grow. It's okay if you still have painful feelings about an experience. You can still have a perspective of growth *and* experience things like sadness, disappointment, anxiety, hurt, or anger.

You should honor the ways that you have changed (and will continue to change) after difficult circumstances. Our challenges make us unique and they can provide important lessons for whatever lies ahead.

Resiliency Recap

The overall way we look at life's struggles is important. We can see challenges as something we want to hide from and avoid, but in the long term, that doesn't help us learn or grow. Cognitive flexibility is the ability to see things from different perspectives—both during and after a challenging situation. Realistic optimism is the ability to plan ahead in a way that keeps you hopeful but grounded.

You can support an optimistic outlook with daily practices that involve humor, fun, joy, and gratitude. Taken together, all of these skills will help you create a daily life that's more enjoyable. When life is really tough, these practices can actually help you feel moments of hope and happiness, even in some of the most difficult times.

Finding Meaning and Purpose

Congratulations on making it to the final skill in this book! You should appreciate all the hard work you've done so far. Take a moment to look back on how many techniques you've added to your resiliency tool box. These are skills that you can use when you really need them—when life throws you a curveball—and you can also use them as a part of your daily life for more energy and focus, and for better relationships. You now know that when you're stressed or feeling anxious, angry, sad, disappointed, or overwhelmed you can:

- Focus on a healthy routine

- Cut back or stop any substance use (alcohol, drugs, smoking or vaping)

- Practice mindfulness

- Use emotional tolerance skills

- Learn from your past mistakes

- Get help for depression and anxiety

- Create safe and healthy connections

- Take healthy chances

- Practice cognitive flexibility and realistic optimism

Once you are doing pretty well on a daily basis—you are taking care of your responsibilities and your relationships—you might want to look at how you can contribute even more to the world. Everything in your life doesn't have to be perfect to figure out some of your deeper values and goals. Unfortunately, the challenges of life keep on coming. You might be experiencing everyday stressors at school, at work, or during class, or maybe you are dealing with uncertainty about the future, abuse, discrimination, or serious illness. The setbacks you've experienced in life may actually give you a lot of perspective as you explore finding *meaning* and *purpose*.

---

mean·ing (Merriam-Webster 2020f)

1: The thing one intends to convey.

2: Something meant or intended; aim.

In terms of resilience, we often try to figure out *why* something happened to us, or the *meaning*. In the previous skill, we saw that cognitive flexibility can help you learn something from what you have gone through. In the case of more serious challenges—like being abused, living through a natural disaster or an accident, or losing a loved one—you may never really understand the meaning of why something happened.

You may find yourself asking questions like, *Why did this happen to me?* and *What did I do to deserve this?* Questions like this may never have an adequate answer. The truth is, really difficult things happen to really good people who don't deserve it. Fortunately, cognitive flexibility may help you form questions like, *Is there anything I learned about myself or my strengths based on this experience?* instead of *Why did this happen?*

Although questions about why terrible things happened may have no answers, questions about how you have changed and what you have learned may be worth asking. These kinds of questions can help you make meaning of your experiences. After we learn from situations, we can see whether they inform what we do in the future—our sense of *purpose*.

---

pur·pose (Oxford University Press 2020b)

1: The reason why something is done or used; the aim or intention of something.

2: The feeling of being determined to do or achieve something.

3: The aim or goal of a person; what a person is trying to do, become, etc.

Purpose involves us looking back at a challenge and figuring out how we might transform what we have learned (*meaning*) into a greater mission (*purpose*).

Resilient people are often able to take setbacks and turn them into opportunities for growth. If you've been through something really significant, this process is called *post-traumatic growth*, because it involves the ability to find deeper meaning and purpose after trauma.

Resilience doesn't just involve taking care of yourself. If you are truly looking for ways to enjoy life, you may want to explore ways to engage with your community—and even the world—on a bigger level. Your experiences make you unique. Your voice makes you unique and deserves to be heard. Resilient people find ways to take their own life experiences, figure out what they've learned, and use challenges to inform the things they care about.

There is no right or wrong time to explore meaning and purpose in your life. However, if you are currently in an unsafe situation, you need to focus on your immediate needs and security (see the Resources section). If you are struggling with symptoms that interfere with your daily life, such as anxiety that keeps you from sleeping, or feeling so down that you don't feel like eating or doing anything you enjoy, you should focus on your daily functioning before you focus on finding deeper meaning and purpose. There will be time for you to explore meaning and purpose after you feel better about your daily life. So don't be worried if you don't feel ready to explore these concepts yet. They will be here for you when you are ready.

Maybe you are struggling to figure out what issues you care about, or how your struggles have impacted you. That's okay. Be patient with yourself and give yourself some time. Sometimes, it takes reflection to get an idea of what you really care about. Take a look at Monica's story.

Surviving the Loss of a Parent: Monica's Story

When Monica was eight years old, her father died of a heart attack. After her dad passed away, her mom made an effort to keep the family active in the community. They received a lot of emotional support from family, friends, and their church.

Monica recently started her sophomore year of high school, and she feels pressured by her guidance counselor to join more extracurricular activities. She feels unsure and confused; since her dad died, her favorite place to be is home with her mom and sisters. Her counselor suggests that Monica think about her own life experiences, look through the school's club list, and see what she might want to try.

As she explores, Monica finds that one of the groups does regular community service: volunteering to help kids in foster care and children with special needs. Monica has always known that losing her dad was the most significant challenge she ever faced. Thinking about it, Monica realizes that the support of her community had been so important in helping her family through those tough years. Monica decides to join the group, hoping that her own story of loss might help other kids who are struggling.

Thinking about what you've been through can help you identify what is important to you. Remember that our values, passions, and interests are always changing. That's perfectly normal. And it keeps life exciting. Every few months, it's useful to look back on what has happened to you and think about any bigger lessons you've learned. The following exercise might help.

TRANSFORMING MEANING INTO PURPOSE

Think of some stressors you've experienced in your life, especially the major ones. You can write them down.

Example: The death of my grandmother, my parents' divorce, being bullied, my dad needing to go to rehab (biggest challenge).

Now, think about some of the everyday stressors you've experienced in the last six months.

Example: My friend group fighting all the time, not making the debate team, my tough math class (biggest everyday stress).

Consider any *meaning* you can derive from these events. Remember, meaning doesn't focus on why these things happened; it can focus on *what you learned* about yourself, your own strengths, or the world around you.

Example: From dad going to rehab—I learned that my dad was brave for facing his addiction.

Example: From my tough math class—I learned I had to do homework every night to keep up with tough subjects.

Now, consider how these lessons may influence your current *purpose* or what you care about. Maybe the big things that have happened have influenced you a lot. You may also find smaller setbacks whose lessons are quite meaningful.

If you're having trouble deciding which lessons feel the most important, picture yourself with a microphone. Pretend for a minute that you aren't embarrassed and you can just spread the message—what you have learned—to everyone. What message is the most important to you? This can help you discover some current passions, or a purpose.

Example: I think tutoring little kids in math would be fun, so that they learn not to give up.

Now that you have thought more about the topics that interest you, there are several ways you can become more involved in your community and the world. We will discuss some specific ways you can use your experience and your voice.

Fundraising, Educating, Community Service, and Activism

Once you find things you care about, there are many ways you can make a difference in the world. There is no right or wrong way. Don't feel pressured that you need to make a huge change. Start small and just see what works for you. The causes you care about will change over time, and so will your involvement.

It is important to find ways to give back because there is lots of evidence that helping other people helps you. It can lower your level of depression and anxiety, make you feel less angry or upset, and increase your self-esteem (Memmott-Elison et al. 2020). So doing things for other people doesn't just help them; it also helps you. Here are some key facts about being active in your community:

- Getting involved in your community can help build your sense of competence because you are mastering specific skills.

- You may feel more confident in other areas of your life, for example, in your academic work or in relationships with friends and family.

- You may develop a sense of closeness and connection to the people you're helping.

- You will start to figure out what causes you really care about.

- You might feel a deep sense of empathy and connection to the world, based on your involvement (Hernantes et al. 2019).

Once you decide which causes and issues give you a sense of purpose, you need to decide what kind of impact you want to make. Sometimes, you might think that raising money for your cause makes sense. At other times, you might want to focus on educating your friends, family members, school, or community about a topic. You might decide that volunteering is a great way to get directly involved with something you care about. Finally, you might decide that norms, laws, and society as a whole need to change, so you might become an activist. Let's take a look at each one of these strategies in more detail.

Raising Funds: Amy's Library

Amy is a fifteen-year-old freshman in high school. She was adopted from China when she was a child. Amy loves her family but also wants to find a way to feel connected to the culture of her birth. She and her parents decide to visit the orphanage she lived in until she was eleven months old. She visits several small village schools on her trip.

When Amy returns home, she begins working with the Asian Students Club to raise funds for a library for one of the schools. The club sponsors events and appeals to the local Chinese American cultural group for donations. In her appeal, Amy includes the photos of two young girls she met in China, and she talks specifically about how the books would positively impact their education. Eventually, Amy raises hundreds of dollars to buy books. It gives her an opportunity to remain connected to China and to the girls she met.

As you can see, donating might involve your own money, but fundraising involves a lot more. It can be an opportunity to connect with others and achieve something specific. Amy was smart because she didn't just ask for money for a library. She included a personal appeal—using specific examples of how the money would positively impact people, with an example of how the money might affect the quality of life of two specific girls (Small, Loewenstein, and Slovic 2007). The next exercise will help you if you are considering fundraising for a cause.

LET'S FUND IT

Think of an issue you are passionate about. Is it an existing organization, or are you raising funds for something specific? Now consider the following:

Is there anyone else your age who might be interested in helping you raise funds?

Are there adults who might want to help your efforts?

How will you publicize your fundraising efforts? Online, with flyers, with an event?

Once you identify some of the specifics, think about how you will appeal to people. Remember that a personal appeal will work best, with specific examples of how the money might help someone.

Fundraising is a great way to get involved in your community. Similarly, you might decide that the causes you care about require community education. Take a look at Luke's example.

Forming a Gay-Straight Alliance: Luke's Story

Luke is a fourteen-year-old freshman who has identified as gay since the fifth grade. Luke came out to his parents in middle school, and while his mother is supportive, his father still struggles to accept Luke. In middle school, Luke tried to hide his sexual orientation, and it led to several very serious episodes of depression. Now that Luke is in high school, he is meeting more LGBTQ students.

Luke and his peers decide to start a gay-straight alliance, and they quickly find a teacher who is interested in sponsoring them. They decide that their first priority is to create some supportive, educational information to be published in the school newsletter.

They want LGBTQ students to know that they aren't alone, and they want everyone to understand that prejudice and bigotry are harmful.

Luke's efforts illustrate that sometimes our most difficult experiences can provide us with the life experience to help others and educate the larger community. The following exercise will help you think about ways you can educate others.

WHAT'S YOUR ELEVATOR SPEECH?

Think about a cause you really care about. Maybe you want people to think more about how they treat others. Maybe you want people to understand why a certain topic is really important. One way to do this is by putting together an *elevator speech*, an effective and persuasive statement that gets your point across quickly—in about the time it takes to ride an elevator. Your argument might include:

- Why people should care about this topic.

- Why it is relevant right now.

- What you want people to know.

- Why you have expertise on this topic, or what you've dealt with in your own life that gives you credibility.

Example: *We've been hearing a lot about immigration lately. I think it's important for people to understand how hard immigrants work and how difficult it can be. It's important to me because I'm the child of immigrants and my mom is working two jobs to raise me and my brothers.*

Once you perfect your short elevator speech, you can make it longer, depending on who your audience is.

The next step is to get your message out there. Experiment with the following:

- Your school or local newspaper

- An online post

- A school assembly

- A community forum

- A church event

- An informal gathering of friends

There is no right or wrong way to educate. Once people know that a topic is important to you, they will start seeking out your help and input. It's a great way to spread the word about things that matter to you.

The next approach involves community service, which is also a way to deepen your connections and commitment to the things you care about.

Caring for Seniors: Tara's Story

Tara is a junior in high school, and her relationship with her mother has always been difficult. Although she tries her best to communicate with her mom, she sometimes feels that her mom is very critical of her grades. Tara loves hanging out with her grandparents, but unfortunately they live across the country. When she was younger, she was able to spend more time with them, but now that her schedule is so busy, her visits rarely last more than a few days.

Recently, Tara has started volunteering at the local retirement community, where she prepares coffee and afternoon snacks, and helps keep the game room organized. After months of volunteering,

Tara has developed bonds with many of the residents—and it has actually deepened her relationship with her own grandparents, because she appreciates some of the struggles they must be facing. She also feels proud to talk to her mom about the things she's doing at the senior center, and her mom encourages her efforts.

Tara's volunteer work is a great illustration of how community involvement can be as fulfilling for the volunteer as it is for the recipient. If you are considering volunteering, the following exercise is for you.

SHOW YOU CARE

You might be wondering whether volunteering is for you. Sometimes it can be scary to walk into a new place, and you might wonder whether you have anything to offer. If you decide to try volunteering, choose something you really care about. Maybe it's a topic you are really passionate about, or it's a group that you want to get to know better. Here are some tips:

- Remember that everyone is nervous when they first volunteer somewhere.

- Read about the mission of the organization and write down two questions you can ask someone in charge if you get the chance. That will make you feel prepared.

- Watch your body language. Take a few deep breaths and smile. Don't cross your arms, and make sure to put your phone away. Good body language will help you feel relaxed and it will put others at ease.

- If you don't know what to say, just listen. As you are helping with tasks (for example, serving food, cleaning up), just ask people how they are, listening attentively to their answers. The more you listen, the more you will learn. As an added bonus, people love good listeners!

Make a deal with yourself that you will volunteer somewhere at least three times before you decide whether it's for you. You need to experience a setting at least a few times to see whether it is a good fit, what you can contribute, and what you can learn.

Volunteering in your community is a great way to get to know people and feel like you are making a real difference in people's lives. Another powerful way you can become involved is through activism. Sometimes you don't just want to change individuals, you want to change society. Take a look at Mona's story.

Life After a School Shooting: Mona's Story

Mona is a sophomore in high school. Just four months ago, three of her classmates were killed in a school shooting. Mona still has nightmares about how they died. Sometimes, she still feels guilty that she got to live and they didn't. Mona is in therapy for depression and post-traumatic stress disorder. Her therapist tells her that her reactions are normal, based on the terrible trauma she experienced.

Despite the significant mental health burden that they are carrying, Mona and her friends decide that they must do something to stop the gun violence epidemic. They don't just want to help their friends, they want Congress to change their gun laws. After forming a plan with her therapist to closely monitor her depression and anxiety, Mona becomes involved in several activist groups and speaks nationally about how gun violence is affecting young people. She becomes an example of how you can advocate for something you care about and still be dealing with significant aftereffects. In fact, activism has become an important pathway that is helping her heal.

Activism can be beneficial for our self-esteem and mental health (Gilster 2012). Activism can be particularly useful if you want to try to change laws, politics, and larger cultural beliefs about an issue. If you are considering activism, take a look at the following exercise.

IF YOU DON'T LIKE IT, CHANGE IT

Activism is useful when you are very passionate about a topic and you can't make the changes you want using fundraising, education, or community service. In other words, you need structures to change in order to get your message heard. Here are some ways you can become an activist:

- Write a letter to your elected leaders about the topic you care about.

- Reach out to local media, including television stations, and ask them to cover your topic.

- Sign up for public comment at local board meetings to get your message heard.

- Arrange to meet your local congressperson and talk to them about why you care so much.

- Attend or arrange rallies and marches, and amplify your message through social media coverage of these gatherings.

As you do these things, make sure you are taking good care of yourself:

- Do something fun or enjoyable every day.

- If you feel anxiety, depression, or stress building up, make sure you talk to a trusted friend or adult, or seek professional help.

- Write out encouraging statements that can help you if you feel discouraged or disappointed during your efforts. For example: *We will measure progress in months and years. I know this won't change in a short time.*

- Make sure you are eating nutritious meals and getting some exercise, especially during times of intense activism.

- Have a friend check in on you once a week to make sure you are taking care of yourself.

Activism is tool a that many teens are using. Generation Z is one of the most active, informed generations. You have lived through a lot of stress, including school shootings, economic and social uncertainty, police brutality, environmental destruction, and a pandemic. What's amazing is to see you make meaning of these difficult experiences and turn them into your purpose. However, you should not feel pressured to become an activist. There are many ways to change laws, norms, and culture. You can find your individual way to express your purpose over time.

Resiliency Recap

Everyone experiences some level of adversity in their life. And you may never fully understand why something challenging or traumatic has happened to you. Fortunately, you can develop the ability to look back and learn lessons—to find *meaning* about who you are, your strengths, and the positive aspects of the world around you. This meaning can help define your *purpose*—the issues you care most about.

There are so many ways to get involved and make a difference, including fundraising, educating people about an issue, volunteering, or becoming an activist for change. These kinds of activities take you from resilience to growth. They give you a deep sense that your life and your experiences matter, and that you have something important to contribute to the world—because you do!

Closing

One of the most important aspects of resilience is finding ways to make meaning of obstacles you have encountered in life, taking good care of yourself emotionally, and not letting setbacks define you. In this book, you have reviewed skills that have focused on four major areas.

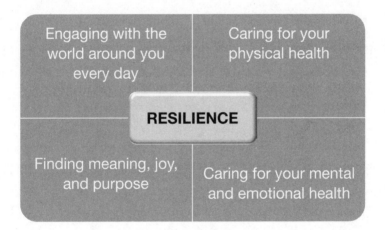

You've made it to the end of this book, so take a moment to congratulate yourself! You've challenged yourself to be open-minded, try new things, and form stronger connections. That is no easy task! You are well on the way in your resilience journey.

Life is full of challenges—big and small. Maybe you're struggling in a hard math class, are moving across town, or just ended a romantic relationship. Or maybe you've dealt with illness, abuse, discrimination, or bullying. The resilience skills you learn can help you during the most difficult times. When you build resilience practices into your daily life, these skills can also help you feel heathier, happier, more energized, and more connected to the world around you! Now you have so many skills to choose from:

- Focus on your *body* by creating a routine that works for you and by limiting your substance use in times of stress.

- Focus on your *mind* by practicing mindfulness and emotional tolerance, learning from mistakes, and treating depression and anxiety.

- Focus on your *connections* by creating a great support system and learning to take healthy chances.

- Focus on your sense of *purpose and meaning* by practicing cognitive flexibility, realistic optimism, and getting involved in your community.

You will create your own recipe for resilience by incorporating something from each area of this square every single day. No journey will look the same. You may run two miles every morning, meditate, talk to your best friend, and volunteer at your local library. Or maybe you decide to quit smoking, talk to a therapist once a week, overcome your fear of public speaking, and create a poetry club at school. Maybe you play basketball, go to church every weekend, hang out with your cousins, and coach the community center preschool sports camp.

The important thing about your journey is that it is uniquely yours, and it is important. You deserve to be treated well and you deserve to be heard. Now you have the skills to deal with those unexpected setbacks and create a life that you truly love. And all those challenges in life will now be a part of your story too—a story of resilience.

Acknowledgments

I am incredibly grateful to every single trauma survivor who has shared their story. Your courage to trust, to connect, and to find meaning and purpose in this challenging world inspires me every day.

Thank you to my teachers and mentors, including Rebecca Campbell, Cheryl Carmin, Michelle Hoersch, Robin Mermelstein, David McKirnan, Joe Stokes, and Erica Sharkansky. You have been an endless source of wisdom and encouragement.

I am grateful to Tesilya Hanauer at New Harbinger Publications, who has been a great source of encouragement over the years. Her insights have been essential in shaping every book that I have written, including this one.

I have no words to properly acknowledge my second-grade teacher, Cynthia Miller, who believed in the potential of every little person who came through her classroom. Without you, Ms. Miller, I may never have found my voice or my purpose.

Thank you to my mother and father, who have modeled empathy and resilience at every step in their lives and mine. I strive to love others the way you do.

Finally, I am grateful for my husband and daughters. Your support is unconditional and forever flexible, from giving me feedback on drafts and providing emotional support to just giving me a good laugh and cooking dinner. Through all of life's ups and downs, I am forever thankful for this amazing family.

Resources

Activism

Black Lives Matter:
      https://blacklivesmatter.com

Environmental Defense Fund:
      https://www.edf.org

Everytown for Gun Safety:
      https://everytown.org/moms

Interfaith Youth Core:
      https://ifyc.org

Southern Poverty Law Center:
      https://www.splcenter.org

Bullying

Stop Bullying:
      https://www.stopbullying.gov/resources/get-help-now

The Trevor Project:
      https://www.thetrevorproject.org

Community Violence and Crime

The National Center for Victims of Crime:
      https://www.victimsofcrime.org

Dating Violence

Break the Cycle:
   http://www.breakthecycle.org

Love Is Respect:
   https://www.loveisrespect.org

The National Domestic Violence Hotline:
   (800) 799-7233 (24-hour hotline),
   https://www.thehotline.org/help

General Resources

ACEs (Adverse Childhood Events) Too High:
   https://acestoohigh.com

Anxiety and Depression Association of America:
   https://adaa.org

National Center for PTSD:
   https://www.ptsd.va.gov

National Suicide Prevention Lifeline
   (800) 273-8255 (24-hour national hotline),
   https://suicidepreventionlifeline.org

Substance Abuse and Mental Health Services Administration:
   (800) 662-4357 (24-hour national hotline),
   https://www.samhsa.gov/find-help/national-helpline

Sexual Assault

National Sexual Violence Resource Center:
   https://www.nsvrc.org

RAINN (Rape, Abuse & Incest National Network):
   https://www.rainn.org

References

Ahola Kohut, S., J. Stinson, C. Davies-Chalmers, E. Ruskin, and M. van Wyk. 2017. "Mindfulness-Based Interventions in Clinical Samples of Adolescents with Chronic Illness: A Systematic Review." *The Journal of Alternative and Complementary Medicine* 23(8): 581–589.

American Psychological Association. 2018. *Stress in America: Generation Z.* Stress in America™ Survey. Washington, DC: American Psychological Association.

Breggin, P. R. 2015. "The Biological Evolution of Guilt, Shame and Anxiety: A New Theory of Negative Legacy Emotions." *Medical Hypotheses* 85(1): 17–24.

Cacioppo, J. T., L. C. Hawkley, and R. A. Thisted. 2010. "Perceived Social Isolation Makes Me Sad: 5-Year Cross-Lagged Analyses of Loneliness and Depressive Symptomatology in the Chicago Health, Aging, and Social Relations Study." *Psychology and Aging* 25: 453–463.

Ekman, P. 1984. "Expression and the Nature of Emotion." In K. Scherer and P. Ekman (Eds.), *Approaches to Emotion*. Hillsdale, NJ: Lawrence Erlbaum.

Felton, J. W., A. Collado, M. Havewala, J. M. Shadur, L. MacPherson, and C. W. Lejuez. 2019. "Distress Tolerance Interacts with Negative Life Events to Predict Depressive Symptoms Across Adolescence." *Journal of Clinical Child & Adolescent Psychology* 48(4): 633–642.

Forgas, J. P. 2014. "Four Ways Sadness May Be Good for You." *Greater Good Science Center,* June, 4.

Gilster, M. E. 2012. "Comparing Neighborhood-Focused Activism and Volunteerism: Psychological Well-Being and Social Connectedness." *Journal of Community Psychology* 40(7): 769–784.

Head, L. S., and A. M. Gross. 2009. "Systematic Desensitization." In W. T. O'Donohue and J. E. Fisher (Eds.), *General Principles and Empirically Supported Techniques of Cognitive Behavior Therapy*. New York: John Wiley & Sons, Inc.

Hernantes, N., M. J. Pumar-Méndez, O. López-Dicastillo, A. Iriarte, and A. Mujika. 2019. "Volunteerism as Adolescent Health Promotion Asset: A Scoping Review." *Health Promotion International.* https://doi.org/10.1093/heapro/daz026.

Iacoviello, B. M., and S. D. Charney. 2014. "Psychosocial Facets of Resilience: Implications for Preventing Posttrauma Psychopathology, Treating Trauma Survivors, and Enhancing Community Resilience." *European Journal of Psychotraumatology* 5(1): 23,970.

Johnston, L. D., P. M. O'Malley, R. A. Miech, J. G. Bachman, and J. E. Schulenberg. 2017. *Monitoring the Future National Survey Results on Drug Use, 1975–2016: Overview, Key Findings on Adolescent Drug Use.* Ann Arbor, MI: Institute for Social Research, University of Michigan.

Kann, L., T. McManus, W. A. Harris, S. L. Shanklin, K. H. Flint, B. Queen, et al. 2018. "Youth Risk Behavior Surveillance—United States, 2017." *Surveillance Summaries* 67(8): 1–114.

Leigh-Hunt, N., D. Bagguley, K. Bash, V. Turner, S. Turnbull, N. Valtorta, and W. Caan. 2017. "An Overview of Systematic Reviews on the Public Health Consequences of Social Isolation and Loneliness." *Public Health* 152: 157–171.

Linehan, M. M. 1993. *Skills Training Manual for Treating Borderline Personality Disorder.* New York: Guilford Press.

Mak, C., K. Whittingham, R. Cunnington, and R. N. Boyd. 2018. "Efficacy of Mindfulness-Based Interventions for Attention and Executive Function in Children and Adolescents—A Systematic Review." *Mindfulness* 9(1): 59–78.

Memmott-Elison, M. K., H. G. Holmgren, L. M. Padilla-Walker, and A. J. Hawkins. 2020. "Associations Between Prosocial Behavior, Externalizing Behaviors, and Internalizing Symptoms During Adolescence: A Meta-Analysis." *Journal of Adolescence* 80: 98–114.

Merikangas, K. R., J. P. He, M. Burstein, S. A. Swanson, S. Avenevoli, L Cui, et al. 2010. "Lifetime Prevalence of Mental Disorders in US Adolescents: Results from the National Comorbidity Survey Replication–Adolescent Supplement (NCS-A)." *Journal of the American Academy of Child & Adolescent Psychiatry* 49(10): 980–989.

Merriam-Webster.com dictionary. 2020a. "Active." *Merriam-Webster.* Accessed May 23, 2020. https://www.merriam-webster.com/dictionary/active.

Merriam-Webster.com dictionary. 2020b. "Cognitive." *Merriam-Webster.* Accessed May 23, 2020. https://www.merriam-webster.com/dictionary/cognitive.

Merriam-Webster.com dictionary. 2020c. "Cope." *Merriam-Webster.* Accessed May 23, 2020. https://www.merriam-webster.com/dictionary/cope.

Merriam-Webster.com dictionary. 2020d. "Flexible." *Merriam-Webster.* Accessed May 23, 2020. https://www.merriam-webster.com/dictionary/flexible.

Merriam-Webster.com dictionary. 2020e. "Guilt." *Merriam-Webster.* Accessed May 23, 2020. https://www.merriam-webster.com/dictionary/guilt.

Merriam-Webster.com dictionary. 2020f. "Meaning." *Merriam-Webster.* Accessed May 23, 2020. https://www.merriam-webster.com/dictionary/meaning.

Merriam-Webster.com dictionary. 2020g. "Resilience." *Merriam-Webster.* Accessed May 23, 2020. https://www.merriam-webster.com/dictionary/resilience.

Merriam-Webster.com dictionary. 2020h. "Social." *Merriam-Webster.* Accessed May 23, 2020. https://www.merriam-webster.com/dictionary/social.

Merriam-Webster.com dictionary. 2020i. "Support." *Merriam-Webster.* Accessed May 23, 2020. https://www.merriam-webster.com/dictionary/support.

Miech, R., J. Schulenberg, L. Johnston, J. Bachman, P. O'Malley, and M. Patrick. 2017. *Monitoring the Future National Adolescent Drug Trends in 2017: Findings Released.* Ann Arbor, MI: Institute for Social Research, University of Michigan.

Min, J. A., Y. E. Jung, D. J. Kim, H. W. Yim, J. J. Kim, T. S. Kim, et al. 2013. "Characteristics Associated with Low Resilience in Patients with Depression and/or Anxiety Disorders." *Quality of Life Research* 22(2): 231–241.

Nhat Hanh, T. 2010. *Peace Is Every Step: The Path of Mindfulness in Everyday Life*. New York: Random House.

Oxford University Press. 2020a. "Mindfulness." Lexico.com. Accessed May 23, 2020. https://www.lexico.com/en/definition/mindfulness.

Oxford University Press. 2020b. "Purpose." Lexico.com. Accessed May 23, 2020. https://www.lexico.com/en/definition/purpose.

Oxford University Press. 2020c. "Shame." Lexico.com. Accessed May 23, 2020. https://www.lexico.com/en/definition/shame.

Pressman, S. D., S. Cohen, G. E. Miller, A. Barkin, B. S. Rabin, and J. J. Treanor. 2005. "Loneliness, Social Network Size, and Immune Response to Influenza Vaccination in College Freshmen." *Health Psychology* 24: 297–306.

Scott-Parker, B. 2017. "Emotions, Behaviour, and the Adolescent Driver: A Literature Review." *Transportation Research Part F: Traffic Psychology and Behaviour* 50: 1–37.

Shadur, J. M., A. L. Ninnemann, A. Lim, C. W. Lejuez, and L. MacPherson. 2017. "The Prospective Relationship Between Distress Tolerance and Cigarette Smoking Expectancies in Adolescence." *Psychology of Addictive Behaviors* 31(5): 625–635.

Shen, L. 2018. "The Evolution of Shame and Guilt." *PLOS ONE*, 13(7).

Shonkoff, J. P., A. S. Garner, B. S. Siegel, M. I. Dobbins, M. F. Earls, L. McGuinn, et al. 2012. "The Lifelong Effects of Early Childhood Adversity and Toxic Stress." *Pediatrics*, 129(1).

Small, D. A., G. Loewenstein, and P. Slovic. 2007. "Sympathy and Callousness: The Impact of Deliberative Thought on Donations to Identifiable and Statistical Victims." *Organizational Behavior and Human Decision Processes* 102(2): 143–153.

Tedeschi, R. G., J. Shakespeare-Finch, K. Taku, and L. G. Calhoun. 2018. *Posttraumatic Growth: Theory, Research, and Applications*. New York: Routledge.

Tilghman-Osborne, C., D. A. Cole, J. W. Felton, and J. A. Ciesla. 2008. "Relation of Guilt, Shame, Behavioral and Characterological Self-Blame to Depressive Symptoms in Adolescents over Time." *Journal of Social and Clinical Psychology* 27(8): 809–842.

Twenge, J. M., B. H. Spitzberg, and W. K. Campbell. 2019. "Less In-Person Social Interaction with Peers Among U.S. Adolescents in the 21st Century and Links to Loneliness." *Journal of Social and Personal Relationships* 36(6): 1,892–1,913.

Uchino, B. 2004. *Social Support and Physical Health: Understanding the Health Consequences of Relationships.* New Haven, CT: Yale University Press.

Wincentak, K., J. Connolly, and N. Card. 2017. "Teen Dating Violence: A Meta-Analytic Review of Prevalence Rates." *Psychology of Violence* 7(2): 224–241.

Sheela Raja, PhD, is an associate professor at the University of Illinois at Chicago. She completed postdoctoral training at the National Center for PTSD, and is a nationally recognized expert on the health effects of trauma and trauma-informed health care approaches. Her other books include *Overcoming Trauma and PTSD*, *The PTSD Survival Guide for Teens*, and *The Sexual Trauma Workbook for Teen Girls*.

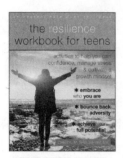

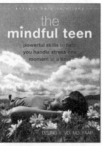